The Fight For My Soul

Swithun English Wright Jr

BALBOA.PRESS
A DIVISION OF HAY HOUSE

Balboa Press books may be ordered through booksellers or by contacting:

Balboa Press
A Division of Hay House
1663 Liberty Drive
Bloomington, IN 47403
www.balboapress.com
844-682-1282

Because of the dynamic nature of the Internet, any web addresses or
links contained in this book may have changed since publication and
may no longer be valid. The views expressed in this work are solely those
of the author and do not necessarily reflect the views of the publisher,
and the publisher hereby disclaims any responsibility for them.

The author of this book does not dispense medical advice or prescribe
the use of any technique as a form of treatment for physical, emotional,
or medical problems without the advice of a physician, either directly
or indirectly. The intent of the author is only to offer information
of a general nature to help you in your quest for emotional and
spiritual well-being. In the event you use any of the information in
this book for yourself, which is your constitutional right, the author
and the publisher assume no responsibility for your actions.

Any people depicted in stock imagery provided by Getty Images are
models, and such images are being used for illustrative purposes only.
Certain stock imagery © Getty Images.

Cover Art by Ziana de Bethune

Scripture quotations taken from the King James Version of the Bible.

Print information available on the last page.

ISBN: 978-1-9822-3635-9 (sc)
ISBN: 978-1-9822-3636-6 (e)

Balboa Press rev. date: 06/02/2021

In loving Memory of Annabell Blanca Wright
March 4, 1946 - September 13, 2016

Contents

1

Spiritual Warfare

My name is Swithun English Wright, Jr. I was born in Brooklyn, but raised in Metropolitan Bronx, New York. My childhood memories take me down a street of many colors— small, three-bedroom homes painted red, blue, gray, and yellow, whose front yards were covered in snow in winter, but sprouted f lowers in summer, lined each side. Our home on Voice Street was sky blue with a porch, but no fence designating our property. All of that color ended abruptly at the threshold. Within were only walls of tan paneling and dark wooden floors varnished to a sheen and immersed in scents of cleaning products and something f loral.

At the corner of Voice Street was a funeral parlor on one side, and Johnny's Bar on the other. I guess if you got stabbed in a rumble at Johnny's, you could skip the middle man and go straight to the funeral parlor. Down that street was a dry cleaner, a hairdresser, Stewart's Deli, and an A & P Supermarket.

And then there was West Side Bowery, Bronx, a totally different story. There were a few clusters of reasonably nice homes, but the rest had deteriorated after the crack era in the 80s. The area consisted mostly of housing projects and rotting dreams. The venomous animosity between West Side Bowery, Bronx and Metropolitan Bronx had sparked many fights, but my generation's would eventually turn deadly!

Onward. I agree with mostly everything platinum-selling rapper Curtis Jackson, aka 50 Cent wrote in his book *From Pieces to Weight: Once Upon a Time in Southside Queens* except this: "Nothing is promised to anyone in this world besides death."

As a Spiritualist, I believe that the one thing in this life of the living that's promised is Heaven or Hell. Heaven, very few get to experience, so to Hell many lost souls are forever bound. Those who are truly spiritual will comprehend, but those who are not will never understand the war over The Chosen One.

While tragically dying from bone cancer, my beloved mother, Annabell B. Wright, shared some insights with my older sister, Mia, who was tending to her. While drifting in and out of consciousness, she revealed that God and Jesus were standing before her. Beyond the Lord there was a war going on between Angels and Demons for the souls of her grandchildren.

To understand her more fully, it's essential to know that Annabell had been born with a gift that enabled her to see and communicate with the dead.

She didn't choose this gift, it chose her. As a child, her mother used to punish her for misbehaving by making her sleep in a room that terrified her. At nine years old— in that dreaded room—she began to experience things that could not be explained.

While lying supine in bed the whole ceiling opened up, and all at once pure daylight flooded the space. Her eyes widened as a strange man with wings descended into the room, frightening her nearly to death. There he remained for timeless, heart-clenching moments as she squeezed her eyes closed, repeatedly praying that he had gone away. However, when she dared to peek again, he was still there.

His image burned itself into her memory. His thick, luminescent wings, tremendous height and power, all of his majestic, Divine self forever seared into her brain. Not yet knowing what an angel was, this Being terrified Annabell to the core of her youthful soul. It was a night she never forgot.

As she got older, these visions didn't cease. In fact, they had become more frequent, seemingly coming at will, while the passage of time allowed her to become more aware of what was happening.

Since her youth Annabell had always read the Holy Bible, and it was in turning to this Book that she obtained insights into her unique situation. On more than one occasion some demonic thing antagonized her by pulling off the covers and yanking at her feet. A Godly Being would intercept to rescue her, adding to her understanding that there was a spiritual warfare playing out before her eyes— that immortal battle between Angels and Demons. She witnessed what some people could only speak about, leaving her no choice but to mature into a good, God-fearing young woman.

At fifteen years old my mother met the love of her life, and that encounter initiated the lifelong test of her faith.

Melvin Clark, a tall, light-skinned fella with wavy black hair, fell madly in love with Annabell. He no sooner proposed to her than he was scheduled to be deployed overseas by the US Army. They promised to reunite and move forward together once he returned.

However, another young man in the neighborhood had his own plan, and watching Annabell marry Melvin wasn't part of it. Who could have known what had been going through Swithun English Wright's mind? He and Annabell had grown up across the street from each other. He'd had plenty of opportunities to get closer to her before Melvin Clark entered the picture, but it seemed that he only really noticed her when some competition stepped in to take her away. Or maybe it was because the color of Annabell's caramel skin was as delicious to him as the shapely body that she had developed. Whatever the reason, he decided he wanted this beautiful young thing for himself, and his mother, his accomplice, helped set the stage for his success.

Immediately after Mr. Clark went into the Army, Swithun slithered in to stake his claim. My mother had no idea what was about to take place. On a beautiful spring afternoon, Swithun's mother, Yellow Bird, spotted Annabell in her yard across the street and took the initiative to invite her over for a visit- most likely, at Swithun's suggestion. The full glory of this bright, sunny spring day seemed to draw something from Yellow Bird's core to her outer hide, a statement of sorts of what she was. Something alluring that couldn't readily be identified as good or evil. The brightness of the day accentuated the high yellow tones of her angular face, and long black hair— physical traits that screamed of her Cherokee ancestry. She stood only about 4'7" but had a powerful presence. Some said she was a "witch." Annabell should have thought twice about that, but she hadn't at the time. She accepted the invitation, not knowing that the chocolate cake she was about to enjoy had been laced with a concoction derived from roots that would cause her to be drawn to a man she did not love— Swithun Wright.

Shortly after Swithun hooked up with Annabell, my oldest brother, Freddie, was born. A year after that, Isabella, my oldest sister, came along followed by Mia. Annabell had three young children by the time she began to recognize wicked things within her marriage.

Swithun began staying out late, drinking, and doing drugs—all activities that received his mother's stamp of approval. Moreover, Yellow Bird couldn't have cared less about his mistreatment of my mother. To make things worse, when my mother was pregnant with her fourth child, vicious rumors were circulating through his family that the child was not his.

My mother went through Hell and grew extremely ill while carrying her fourth child. There were all kinds of weird things going on around her pregnancy that could not be explained. The stress was so much on her that she eventually had a miscarriage.

It wasn't until my mother met a woman that could read the future that things became clear. This woman informed Annabell that she was involved in spiritual warfare and that her mother-in-law had engaged in witchcraft to get her into a relationship with Swithun.

My mother, still young and new to spiritual warfare, just wanted to get out of Brooklyn and away from my father's family, especially his mother.

In the summer of 1967, Annabell f inally convinced Swithun to move to Voice St. They moved into a lovely, sky blue, single-family home with a basement and a wooden porch. They were the first people of color to live on the block.

The neighbors were kind to my family, and my parents' relationship began to improve tremendously. My mother got pregnant with her fifth child, and soon afterward, my father reverted back to his shenanigans—drinking and staying out late.

In one of his drunken stupors, he turned on the gas stove with no flame ignited, and staggered off to bed. Everyone was sound asleep when something struck my mother firmly on her arm, jarring her awake. Groggily, she squinted against the neon lights flowing in through the window, becoming fully awake as an apparition appeared before her. It was the Angel she had seen when she was a child, except this time instead of having wings, he wore a white, three-piece, double-breasted suit with gold buttons. As he pointed toward the hallway, the very distinctive odor of hydrogen sulphide gas lambasted her.

She frantically shook my father, "Swithun, Swithun, wake up!"

He slightly raised his head to see what was going on, as my mother flung open the bedroom windows.

"Don't turn on any lights!" Annabell shouted as he got out of the bed. She knew that if he flicked a switch, the entire house would go up in flames. After opening all the windows in the house, she turned the knob of the stove to off, and called the fire department as a precaution. Thank God everyone was okay, but that wasn't the last time this kind of thing happened.

On another occasion, the very same Guardian Angel woke my mother up again and pointed to the hallway. This time, instead of smelling gas, it was smoke. My father, in his drunken state, had left a pot of hot dogs on the stove before falling asleep. It was like living in Brooklyn all over again.

My mother endured some tough times during her pregnancy with me—a situation that was made much worse when Yellow Bird began circulating rumors that Swithun wasn't the baby's father. She lost tissue and bled almost the entire nine months that she carried me. The doctors warned her that I wouldn't make it.

And then she had a dream. She was walking in a hot desert up a dome of sand. She could feel the heat beneath her feet, and it was real. As she got closer to the top, there stood the Lord King Jesus. Jesus extended his hand and said, "Annabell, I am Jesus. Come and walk with me." He walked with my mother toward a hut that was so purely white, its brilliance hurt her eyes. When the Lord opened the door, there lay a dark-skinned baby boy with curly hair.

Jesus stated, "This is yours and Swithun's son."

As my mother came awake, her feet were still hot from walking through the desert. It had not been just a dream. No way. She shook my father out of his sleep, declaring, "Swithun, Swithun! Our son is going to live!"

He mumbled, "No, Annabell. You know what the doctors said. The baby is not going to make it."

"No! Get up! You need to hear my dream!" She forced him to hear her out, and he still did not believe.

Be that as it may, Annabell continued suffering through the same bad symptoms of bleeding, and loss of tissue from her womb. She suffered the entire nine months, but she knew her child would live. She knew because Jesus had said so, and that was enough for her. The Lord King Jesus didn't lie.

On April 6, 1968, I came into this world. Despite Grandma Wright's rumors of me being another man's child, I was the spitting image of my father. I came into this world looking exactly the way my mother had seen me in her dream in the straw hut in the desert. I was born a healthy, dark-skinned baby boy with a curl down the middle of my head. I was also the f irst newborn in the new house my parents had bought.

My father had never quite grown accustomed to my mother seeing spirits. It rattled his cage. Anytime one of them startled her awake if he wasn't passed-out-drunk, he pretended to be asleep. She'd shake him to try and get his attention, but he would not budge—never considering the reality that the spirit knew very well whether he was asleep or pretending.

If that wasn't disturbing enough, Annabell began to see spirits during the daytime, as well.

It was broad daylight, and my parents were taking a nap while I slept in my crib on the other side of the bedroom. All at once, my mother jolted upright, startled by the spirit of an elderly White woman creeping towards my crib. The spirit's focus was clearly on me, but she was also on high alert for Annabell's reaction. As my mother got out of bed, the spirit raced out of the room. Unrattled by what was now commonplace to her, Mom went back to sleep.

Having no success the first time, the spirit returned a few days later with two more spirits, and hovered around my crib. Accustomed to seeing ghosts, Annabell was not alarmed, and since these did not seem to have ill intentions, she dozed off to sleep. Upon awakening again, my mother noted that my crib was surrounded by spirits who seemed to be engaged in a discussion.

This paranormal activity continued as time went on. There were spirits around me, regardless of what I was doing, or what time of day or night it was. Eventually, other strange events began to unfold in the house.

One night, my father came home late to a man in a long black trench coat in our dining room. He appeared to be on the phone. So real was he that my father pulled out a small chrome .25 semi-automatic pistol and yelled, "What the hell are you doing in my house?!"

The man glanced toward him, smiled, and then ran into the kitchen with my father chasing him. My father continued his pursuit as the spirit flashed down into the basement. He looked at my father, issuing another sarcastic grin. Pops fired two shots at him. Laughing, the spirit turned away from my father and ran through the wall.

The gunshots awakened my mother, who jumped out of bed and ran down the stairs. She screamed, "Swithun, what the hell is going on?"

She thought he was drunk, until he responded tremulously, "Annabell, you ain't gonna believe this." Straight-faced and sober, he relayed his experience to her, and she knew he was telling the truth.

By this time, Annabell was well aware that she had a Guardian Angel and that she could see spirits. However, Swithun's experience that night was what it had taken to dissolve any doubt that he had about the events his wife said were going on in this house.

That was just the beginning. Eventually, something much deeper would unfold within these walls.

2

Out of Body Experience

On a cold winter night, my mother awakened from her sleep feeling thirsty. Kissing Dad on the forehead, she left him resting peacefully and headed downstairs for a cold glass of water.

Flicking on the kitchen light, she was jolted by the sight of my father, in his pajamas, standing in front of the open refrigerator. She closed her eyes and shook her head, as if she is having a bad dream, but when she looked again, he was still there, pouring himself a glass of water. Annabell *knew* that Swithun was still asleep in bed, where she had left him. Or *was* he? What in the world was going on?

She studied him closer. He appeared to be in a world of his own, because he didn't look toward her, or utter a single word.

She wheeled around and raced back upstairs. "Swithun, Swithun wake up! Honey, where are you?" Clearly, he was right where she had left him, his form dimly illuminated by the streetlight f iltering in through the curtains.

"I'm in the kitchen getting something to drink," he mumbled.

My mother was taught by her grandmother that if someone's soul walks out of their body you must give that soul time to reenter the body before waking them up or else they'll die. Mom stepped back and gawked at him, as the soft sound of snoring whispered across the semi-darkness.

She grabbed her Bible off the nightstand and sat on the edge of the bed to read Scripture, but then she paused and set the book aside as her thoughts drifted to the wall in the basement. What *was* it about this house?

In the spring of 1968, a distinguished gentleman named George Hawkins, a Vietnam Veteran, gifted Annabell with a well-trained, all-black German Shepherd from the war. The dog itself was an honorable war Vet, and the bond between this man and his long-time friend was a deep one. However, Mr. Hawkins had lost a leg, and wasn't able to care for his trusted friend anymore. When Mr. Hawkins turned Spook over to Mom, the poignancy of this moment etched itself forever into her memory.

The old soldier, got down on one knee, grabbed Spook's face with both hands, gazed deeply into his eyes, and spoke quietly, "Now Spook, this is Annabell, your new owner. You must obey her." The man and his dog stared at each other, knowing that an understanding had been reached, even as the pain of letting go clearly tore at both of them.

Annabell felt honored to have been the one he chose to care for Spook. She brought him and this memory home with her.

Anytime company arrived, Spook made it his business to sit in between the visitors and his new owner. If they maneuvered in a manner toward her, he'd growled at them with fangs bared, to establish their boundaries, and made it very clear that those boundaries were not negotiable. *Keep your distance.*

My mother was amazed at how smart this dog was, and took very good care of him, just as she had promised.

One Saturday afternoon, when she was walking Spook around the neighborhood to do his business, they came across a broken radio in the street. Spook jumped in front of her, making her stop in her tracks, and began barking frantically.

Annabell tugged on his leash, but he wouldn't let up. It took only seconds for her to realize that this dog, just as it was with so many human soldiers, suffered from PTSD — Post Traumatic Stress Disorder. To Spook this broken radio with its cracked parts and loose wires was a bomb threatening their lives. Annabell had to literally drag him away from it, which was no easy feat with a Shepard that strong.

He was by far the best guard dog she'd ever owned. She felt safe with Spook in the house because he was very protective of her, not to mention he was trained to attack.

When Pops stayed out late partying it didn't matter because Spook protected the house. He normally sat at the foot of her bed, and she felt safe with him there.

One particular evening, his ferocious barking awakened her. Oddly, he was not at the foot of the bed, but somewhere else in the house. She snatched her robe off a nearby chair and put it on before retrieving a hammer out of the top drawer of the nightstand. Armed with a hammer, she continued calling for Spook, as she cautiously crept her way down the stairs following the sound. What was wrong? She called out, "Spook! Spook, come here boy!"

Normally, he would stop what he was doing and come to her, but not this time. As she entered the kitchen, she noticed that the basement door was slightly ajar which baffled her because she always made sure it was shut before going to bed. She stood at the top of the stairs and called for him one more time, "Spook! Spook come here boy!"

He continued barking, growling, and scratching, leaving her with no choice but to go down into that basement. When she reached the bottom of the stairs, she found Spook up on his hind legs, scratching and gouging through the sheetrock—on the same wall my father had seen a ghost run through. He had scratched a hole right through to the concrete, with now-bloody paws.

Had he too witnessed something passing through that wall? She hurried back up the stairs to get Spook's leash, and returned to the basement, where she hooked it onto his collar and forced him to come up to the kitchen. Locking the basement door, she urged Spook to come up to the second floor. Against his will, he obliged, but wouldn't stop barking and growling toward the staircase. Annabell hooked his leash to a radiator in her room and told him to stay put.

When my father got home, she explained to him what she'd witnessed. Dad, with his pistol in his hand, went down the stairs to check out the basement. He wanted to ensure that there was no one inside the house with them. Once in the basement, his eyes widened, as the sensations of anxiety crept into his body. As Annabell had described, there was a huge hole in the sheetrock, with stains from Spook's bloodied paws, and scratches on the concrete wall just behind it. He returned to the bedroom, shaking and scratching his head in disbelief.

"That dog did that to the wall?" he asked Mom, while standing in front of the bed with both hands on his hips.

"Yes Swithun, I saw it with my own eyes!"

"Annabell, this house was built on something terrible" he replied, staring at Spook, who was now resting peacefully by the radiator.

"Things have gone too far" he said.

What could she say? He was right. She nodded. But what could they do about it? Not much.

These paranormal events continued. The harmless spirits that visited me from time to time had grown comfortable inside the house. They no longer ran if my mother caught them. The spirit of a short, White, elderly woman often visited and sat on her bed after peeking in on me in my crib. This spirit silently smiled at my mother for a few moments, and then faded away. Mom became used to it.

In February of 1969, a Nor'Easter category 2 storm hit New York City causing chaos and disruption throughout. Thousands of travelers became stranded on roads and at the airports. At least ninety-four people lost their lives in the storm, and my family lost Spook.

Someone had let Spook out in the yard to potty and the backyard gate was open. Spook took off into the severe storm and never returned. Annabell wandered through the storm, calling his name, but to no avail. He was gone. My mother was devastated, wandering around with a shattered heart for a very long time. She told us kids that when dogs were about to die, they distanced themselves from their loved ones. My siblings and I believed it to be true.

Being raised in a house with eight siblings was the best. There was always someone around to play with, talk to, and care for. And we all protected each other, from the time we were kids right into maturity.

When I was younger, it seemed like Mom was always pregnant. One after another, I always had someone new to play with. Mom did her best to make sure we always had a wonderful Christmas. My sisters had all kinds of dolls. One year they received a kitchen set with an oven that baked real cakes. I remember Freddie, the oldest of all of us, playing with his race car set while my younger brother and I enjoyed our Tonka trucks and little green army soldiers. We even had the green plastic airplanes and helicopters to match. Whether we got a little or a lot we were a tight and happy family.

As the years went on, my mother continued to suffer verbal abuse from Grandma Wright. There was always something negative insinuated about Mom being pregnant with another man's child. Even as a young boy I couldn't understand why Grandma Wright behaved this way. Annabell was a good woman. Even after she had discovered that witchcraft had been used to get her and my father together, she still tried to love him.

Eventually, my father walked out on us. The drunken fool left Mom after she had nine children by him. My mother stood her ground, and never lost faith in God. She used to gather us around her bed, on our knees, and then teach us Scriptures from the Holy Bible. Although times got really bad for us, Annabell made certain we put God in our hearts—and trust me, times got *really* hard.

We had to share a box of grits and one stick of margarine at times, but all nine of us somehow got to eat. There were times when my father would come by and drop off some money or food, but it didn't change the fact he wasn't with us.

Grandma Wright continued to be an evil bitch towards my mother on a regular basis. She'd instigate fights between my parents by encouraging my father to treat Mom badly. If that wasn't bad enough, when Grandma Wright came to visit our house, she would plant roots—another form of witchcraft. It was already terrible that the house was built on some kind of gateway for spirits to pass through our home, so we really didn't need Grandma Wright making it worse. The evils Grandma Wright would plant in the house brought a lot of bad luck. My mother was a blessed, God-fearing woman from the start, so the logical conclusion was that the battle was against her spiritually.

Annabell had her weakness for my dad, because every now and then she allowed him to move back in. He would be half-decent for a while, but always reverted back to his old drunken, disrespectful ways. He would drink and invite his friends over to play cards all night. Things got ugly when one of his friends said something very inappropriate towards my oldest sister. My mother went off like a bomb. She flipped the table over where my father and his friends were playing cards and drinking, and told them all to get out of her house, including my father.

Shortly afterward, he returned and revealed to my mother that he'd sold his soul to the devil, but Mom was having none of it. She knew that Jesus was much more powerful than Satan, so she called on the Blood of Jesus as she had taught us to do.

"Jesus is Lord of us all!" she shouted repeatedly before sending my father on his way.

Before leaving he confessed to keeping her pregnant on purpose so that no other man would want her. Although broken-hearted, she would not let us down. There were times when my mother's mother, Grandma Royce, did help us, but it came with a price. In exchange for the help Mom had to clean her house from time to time.

Grandma Royce was no saint. She was verbally abusive issuing snide comments such as "Why did you have all these kids?" Comments like that only added to the strain that Mom was already experiencing while trying to raise nine kids by herself. Every now and then I would hear one of her friends suggesting, "Annabell put them in a shelter until you get yourself together."

That notion never crossed my mother's mind and for the love of Jesus—she'd never do such a thing. No matter what we were going through, she would not let someone's opinion become reality for her. Mom kept us rooted in the Bible and attending church regularly. That's the way we were raised.

There was no other choice but for my mother to get help from public assistance in the form of food stamps and Medicaid for me and my siblings. Freddie, the oldest, and I, had to become men at an early age.

The deli around the corner was owned by Mr. and Mrs. Stewart who originated from the Virgin Islands. They were a Christian couple who knew of our family's struggles, so out of compassion they gave Freddie and me after school jobs to generate incomes. Freddie was thirteen and I was only eight years old at the time. We were fast learners and did a little bit of everything at the deli from stocking shelves to replenishing the beverage supplies to sweeping and mopping f loors.

On the weekends we did much more and worked longer hours. Before long, Mrs. Stewart had me helping her clean their home above the deli on Saturdays. She taught me how to dust furniture, wash walls, and vacuum the carpet. She fed me on my breaks—excellent West Indian food like peas and rice with oxtails smothered in gravy. Mrs. Stewart also made a mean coconut bread from scratch that I loved to wash down with a Caribbean beverage. She always gave me a choice of four: Champagne Cola, Iris Moose, Caribbean Vanilla Shake, or Peanut Butter Shake. I was also crazy about the Jamaican beef patties stuffed between some fresh Cocoa Bread, but there was nothing like those West Indian home-cooked meals of hers.

The Stewarts were good to us. We not only ate well at the deli, but made money to bring home to provide food for the rest of our family.

3

Evil Visitors

We may have been poor in finances, but we were rich in blessings. Every evening our mother continued to gather us around her bed for prayer, and afterward, captivated our interest with some very intriguing ghost stories.

One of my personal favorites was a story about our great-grandparents, Captain Bill Royce and Cynthia Royce. Captain Bill was a blue-eyed, blonde-haired German, and Cynthia was a pretty, dark-skinned lady. They made their living running moonshine through the southern state of Georgia back in the 1930's when alcohol was illegal, and the penalty was usually hanging to death.

Captain Bill, accompanied by the feisty and loyal Cynthia, had used a buggy pulled by four horses to transport their moonshine along dirt roads, through the darkness of night, since there were no streetlights.

During their travels, they had to cross a bridge. The McCarthy Bridge in Macon Georgia was nicknamed "Killer Crossing". Strange things were reported after several black moonshine runners were caught crossing the bridge, and hung by a noose from it. According to Mom, when Captain Bill's horses came to the threshold of the bridge, they would rear up and come to a sudden halt.

Captain Bill would dismount the buggy and argue with the unseen. "I'm not giving you nothing tonight! I had it with all of you! Enough!" Whatever it was, it wouldn't let the horses get by.

Running late to his destination, Great-Grandpa Royce would start cursing those spirits something terrible. Then, he would grab a bottle of moonshine, go to the edge of the bridge, and pour the moonshine on the ground. Great-Grandma Royce said you could hear the ghosts sucking up the moonshine. Once they'd finished, the horses would settle down, and they would finally be allowed to cross the bridge.

Mom was a good storyteller. When we weren't listening to them, we enjoyed other activities. Freddie loved to play-fight with all of us, which taught us how to defend ourselves. He used to tell us stories too, about the gangs in the neighborhood.

Two of the well-known gangs were the Black Spades and Seven Crowns. It was in the early 1970's when my brother had witnessed several rumbles between the two. He explained that there was a code of honor between the gangs—an agreement, or a set of rules—when it came to rumbling. No guns or knives were allowed when fighting. He claimed to have seen twenty or thirty members on each side engaged in hand-to-hand combat. They'd fight for a long time before the cops arrived.

I remember my mother having plenty of friends. She'd embrace everyone, regardless of their walk of life. Mom was friendly with the Coleman sisters, Kay, Gloria, and Rose. They lived next door to Cee Cee, a single mother with two kids. Next to her were Mr. and Mrs. Miller.

Of all the people that Mom was friendly with, a lady named Cutie was her best friend. Cutie had a heavy southern Alabama accent, and always came bearing gifts. She would bring us toys, cookies, and candy. The sound of her voice excited all of us and made us happy.

Unfortunately, all of that changed one night. Mom was at Cee Cee's house playing cards while my brothers and I were at home lying on the bed we shared talking and playing around. We were just doing what kids did when Mom wasn't around.

I was nine years old at the time. Amell was eight, and our youngest brother was three. We were supposed to be asleep at that hour, but obviously, we were not. We heard Cutie's deep southern voice calling out for our Mom one time, very loud.

"Annabell!"

We shouted, excitedly, "Cutie! Cutie's here!"

She didn't come up the stairs. When I turned and looked at my brothers they had both fallen asleep- just like that.

What happened next was the most frightening moment in all of my nine years. Out of mid-air, a tall, White gentleman in a white Doctor's coat appeared next to me, standing beside the bed. Seconds later, a short, elderly White woman appeared next to him, and was soon followed by the appearance of a dark, hooded monk, who seemed to be faceless.

The monk floated toward me. I covered my face, but peeked at them between my fingers. Although my heart hammered from fear, I lowered my hands to stare at them, while they stared down at me. Those moments seemed to drag on forever.

I recall having a sore on my ear from scratching a mosquito bite. The doctor leaned over me, and with his index finger, gently touched my sore. Seconds later, the elderly woman and the monk disappeared, leaving me alone with the Doctor and my sleeping brothers. All he did was stare at me.

Everyone else in the house had to be asleep as well, because my mother and Cee Cee came to the front door and began knocking, but no one was awake to let them in- Nor did anyone hear the knocking, which was odd.

"Mommy! Mommy!" I screamed at the top of my lungs. "What? What the fuck is it?" I heard my mother scream as she and Cee Cee tried to break the door down but couldn't.

Mom grabbed something nearby and broke the porch window. Cee Cee crawled through and opened the door for her. Meanwhile, I got out of bed and stood before the tall doctor. I was looking up and he was staring down at me, as my mother was making her way up the stairs. I heard someone as clear as the blue sky saying, "You can run through him, Swithun! You can run through him!"

I walked right through the doctor, and then turned and stared at him. He glanced over his shoulder, and smiled. As my mother hit the top stairs, he faded into thin air. My mother yelled, *"What the fuck is it?!"*

"Did you see him?! Huh, Ma? Did you see him?"

"See who?" She softened her tone as I collapsed, utterly terrified, into her arms.

I explained to my mother exactly what had happened, and she listened. Meanwhile, Cee Cee had put out a small f ire downstairs. One of my older sisters had hung some clothes to dry in front of the oven, and they had caught fire. This blaze had been igniting even as I was being frightened out of my mind by apparitions. That is when I started to believe that God is on time, every time.

Later that evening, when things quieted down, my mother told me about the visitation she had had with an angel, when she was nine. She explained to me that angels came to her frequently, and that she saw them all the time... and she was surprised to discover that her gift had been passed down to me.

She also reminded me of the story about her visitation with the Lord King Jesus in the desert, who had shown her visions to assure her that I would come into this world alive and healthy, regardless of the doctors' warnings to the contrary. Before going to bed, she reminded me of all of our spiritual encounters, including the spirits surrounding my crib. It was a lot for a 9-year-old to take in and it concerned me. By the following day, the sore on my ear had healed, and it was back to life as I knew it—school all day and my after-school job at Stewart's Deli in the evenings and on weekends.

Mr. and Mrs. Stewart had a nephew named Rico. One day at work, Rico and I were spying on the customers— that is, peering through the glass doors of the refrigerator from inside. Mr. Stewart had very keen intuition. When he suspected something devious about to transpire in his store, he'd go to the shelves where the cleaning products were displayed, open a bottle of ammonia, and sprinkle a bit of it around. He usually did this right before Rico and I caught someone trying to steal, and that usually put an end to that notion.

Later that evening, when I mentioned what I witnessed to my mother, she explained to me how wicked spirits don't like ammonia- that they ran from it. She taught me that although wicked spirits didn't like ammonia, I should use the Holy Bible f irst, when it came to dealing with the supernatural.

As time went on, she educated me on additional weapons that I could use against the enemy in spiritual warfare. She taught me certain things to do when the devil interfered with God's children. Meanwhile, Grandma Wright continued on with her evil assaults toward my mother, and things got a lot worse.

We got another dog named Choo-Choo, a mixed breed. My mother began to notice strange behavior in our new pet. Choo-Choo was hard of hearing. She couldn't hear anyone walking about outside, or even a car engine running. Mom eventually noticed that every night, shortly after midnight, Choo-Choo started growling at the basement door. This behavior went on until the night that someone accidentally left the basement door open.

My mother awoke to the sound of Choo-Choo barking, growling, and ripping at something. As always, everyone else was asleep when Mom grabbed her hammer before venturing downstairs. As she approached the basement door, the sound of Choo-Choo's growling intensif ied.

She slowly descended the stairs, to witness once again, what she had seen almost nine years prior. Choo-Choo was trying to power her way through that wall. It was as if something was playing peekaboo with the dog, and she didn't like it. Just as it had been with Spook, Choo-Choo had scratched her away through the repaired sheetrock, and was bleeding at her two front paws from clawing at the concrete.

It was no small feat for Mom to get Choo-Choo under control. We older siblings knew enough to understand what was happening when we saw the wall downstairs, and the mess that the dog had caused. After hearing my mother's ghost stories, it hadn't taken a Rocket Scientist to figure out what had transpired.

Something was in, or beyond, that damned wall.

My mother grew weak for my father now and then and always tried *one more time*, as he had occasionally seemed to want to do right by us. However, Grandma Wright continued to stir the pot until the marriage finally fell apart for good.

It was def initely over for Swithun when Mom met another man who treated her with respect. Jacob Davis not only respected Mom, but generously contributed food and money, as our needs required. He didn't mind helping even though we weren't his biological children.

When Grandma Wright found out, she dug into her bag of dirty tricks. My father and Grandma Wright paid us a visit while Jacob wasn't there. Mom was suspicious of their unexpected visit, but felt obligated to let them in, solely because of us kids. They came bearing gifts and food to throw us off of the real reason for their visit. Something of great evil came through that door with them but Mom couldn't pinpoint it at the moment.

While my mom was preoccupied with us and my father, Grandma Wright asked to use the bathroom. When she returned from upstairs, she wanted to leave immediately. She raced out the door with Pops close behind. My mother searched everywhere upstairs to see if Grandma Wright had dropped anything unusual, but couldn't f ind anything.

As usual, Jacob would come in on the weekends after working at Jersey Raceway, where he groomed horses. That Saturday evening, he was well when he entered the house, but shortly afterward, Jacob became extremely ill. By the end of the night he didn't even look like the same person who had come through the door earlier.

My mother grabbed a Holy Bible and began to pray. While she prayed, I experienced a powerful urge to go up to their bedroom, and over to the radiator. I stood in front of it for a while, and then reached inside of it and pulled out a big wad of aluminum foil. Inside of the foil was a bone, which turned out to be a shoulder bone from a male corpse. That evening a friend of Mom's rushed over and gave Jacob a spiritual bath.

The next day he was perfectly fine, but upset that my mother hadn't warned him about my father's and grandmother's visit. Jacob knew they were evil, but they caught him off guard that day. Jacob also had a spiritual gift, which was why I could see how he and my mother clicked. My mother had said that Jacob was a "Clairvoyant." In Jacob's case, his gift was the ability to focus on a person, place, or thing, and determine where it was. She also believed, and taught us, that no human had the ability that the Almighty God has. Glory to God always!

Mom told me that Jacob would call her up at times, and tell her exactly what she was doing. On one occasion Jacob called and told her to stop yelling at us kids. He even knew what her yelling was about. It was something that happened from time to time as my mother's spiritual battle started to come full circle.

4

Family Love

In the early '70's, Mom befriended a short Jewish woman from Bayside, Bronx whose name was Ida. Ida was able to read the future. On a beautiful, clear summer day, Mom and Ida were enjoying a nice, cool drink on the front porch, watching the world go by, when Ida revealed to Annabell, "You're under spiritual attack by the hand of your Mother-in-law."

"What?" she asked hardly surprised. It wasn't anything Annabell didn't already suspect, but maybe something she had needed to hear, or have aff irmed in some way.

"Annabell, you were meant to marry Melvin Clark. He was to be your true love."

Annabell shifted her gaze thoughtfully toward the sky as Ida went on to explain how Swithun had used black magic to bring the two together. As if reading Annabell's mind, Ida continued, "The marriage wasn't ordained by our Creator, was it?"

"No." Annabell admitted. With Annabell being blessed and Swithun Wright being cursed, it was a perfect breeding ground for spiritual warfare. "I think Yellow Bird Wright knew I was a blessed and Godly woman, and tried to undermine that by constantly spreading rumors that I was pregnant with another man's child. Since she's not a God-fearing person, she doesn't understand the reasons for my blessings."

Ida said, "Yellow Bird and Swithun Wright are spawns from hell and will always be."

Ida finished her drink and went on her way, explaining that she had errands to run, and leaving Annabell with that information to process. It was nearly overwhelming considering she was relatively new to such a concept as spiritual warfare. Her life was a struggle, what with nine children by Swithun, and a newborn baby with Jacob. These thoughts of the timeless battle of Good Vs. Evil unfurling in the unseen background of her life, on top of these already difficult times, gave her more to ponder than she had time for most days.

Grandma Wright just would not cease with her witchcraft, and my father continued visiting without prior notification—sometimes while my mother wasn't home. I was about eleven years old when he stopped by, uninvited, while Mom was out grocery shopping. He went upstairs to use the bathroom, and moments later, called me upstairs to join him.

When I got there, he was standing in front of the sink, staring into the mirror, and instructed me to stand beside him, and do the same.

"Okay, son I need you to just look in the mirror and stay still." He said, as he began to recite some kind of demonic chant.

Scared out of my wits, I muttered, *"W-what?"*

The bathroom door swung open, and Mom blasted in like a thunderbolt, *"Swithun!* What are you *doing?!* "* Without waiting for my father to answer, she yanked me out of the bathroom, unaware of how far he'd gotten with his evil deed.

The floor boards resounded as my father raced out of the bathroom, down the stairs, and out of the house. Mom shouted out the bedroom window, as he ran up the block. "Get the fuck out of my house! You would curse your own blood!"

Mom continued yelling and cursing until he turned the corner and disappeared from sight. The fury in her eyes softened as she turned toward me and pulled me in for a comforting hug, meant to soothe the terror that she knew burnt through my soul. Mom grabbed the Bible off of her nightstand, closed her eyes, and began a silent prayer over me, before sending me to bed.

Things had gotten slow at Jersey Raceway. Jacob decided to take Mom away for the weekend, and left us kids at home. Dad had not been around for a while, but it was almost as if he knew that Mom and Jacob were gone, because he came by, uninvited, again.

This time, he was not alone. He brought his cousin, Briar, who was short and dark-skinned, with an intimidating scar on his forehead. Everyone called him "Bry."

My father asked, "How would you like to go with us to Bry's house, and DJ?"

Being with my father was completely the opposite of when I was with Mom. It was always a lot of fun, and at times adventurous. Bry was a Disc Jockey, and I was excited to be invited to his house to play around with the DJ equipment. They both knew that I was in love with music, so I was thrilled to go.

Cousin Bry lived alone in a part of Bronx that was very close to Brooklyn in a well-furnished, three-bedroom, two-bathroom house. He had a trained German Shepherd. Since it was my first time seeing the dog, Bry introduced us as if it was human.

Later that night, after we played music and ate pizza, Bry ordered the dog to guard me while he and my father went out to "take care of some business." My father promised they wouldn't be gone long, but they were gone long enough for me to fall asleep on Bry's bed watching television with the dog at my feet.

When they returned, Bry woke me up and asked me to come downstairs. The dog followed us. Bry grabbed the dog's leash, and hooked it to his collar. He told me to watch as he commanded the dog to roll over, sit up and lay down. I thought it was the coolest dog ever. Bry had it so well trained.

Shortly after Bry entertained me with the dog show and all, my old man sent me to bed for the night. He and Bry were downstairs drinking beer, and I heard them talking until I fell asleep.

Later I woke up thirsty so I headed down the stairs to get something to drink. Halfway down the stairs I began to hear loud snorting. Unaccustomed to this lifestyle, I didn't know what to think when I hit the third step from the bottom and found myself witnessing one of the biggest drug scenes in my life. My eyes widened at the sight of my old man scooping up white stuff from the table in a single playing card and holding it to his nose.

I tiptoed down the last couple of steps to get a better view. There were stashes of drugs in large plastic bags, and there were little plastic bags as well containing white powder. I noticed a long black gun on the table in front of my old man, and Bry also had a shotgun on the f loor by his feet. I had never seen anything like this except on TV.

When they noticed me staring at them, Pops yelled, "Boy, what you want?"

"I wanted… a drink of juice." I whispered, fearfully. "Get your ass back upstairs and I'll bring it to you!" Pops ordered. I turned tail and ran back up the stairs, my mouth dryer than before.

My mother came back into town, and f lipped out on my older siblings for letting me go with my father. When Pops and Bry brought me home, it got ugly. She cursed him out for taking me without her permission, and began hurling things at my father and Bry. After they bolted from there, she interrogated me at length, wanting to know everything, especially if he had brought me to see Grandma Wright.

I came clean and told her what had happened. She was steamed over the whole ordeal, and went on to explain to me how wicked my father and his family were. She felt that exposing me to guns and drugs was a form of cursing me, and maybe she was right, but I was too young to understand at the time.

My mother and Jacob continued taking weekend trips while leaving my oldest brother, Freddie, in charge. Freddie was a mean son-of-a-gun. He ran the house like a hard-assed prison guard. He and I would always get into some kind of debate, no matter what it was about. Being that he was the oldest, he felt he was always right.

Freddie also made sure he got more than his fair share of food before everyone else was served. For instance, whenever we had franks and beans, Freddie would take five franks out of the ten. Even when he'd dish out cookies or any other snacks, he'd get the lion's share of that too. It really drove me crazy, but what bothered me the most was when he drank straight out of the milk carton before anyone else could get to it. That made my skin boil.

I was around thirteen years-old when I started rebelling against the rules, and was also old enough to escape my brother's dictatorship. I couldn't take it anymore, so when some of my first cousins moved from Brooklyn to Part Of Me Ave. in Bronx, their home became my refuge. In that group were my Auntie Cheryl and six children, namely, Noah and his younger brother, Jack, and their four sisters, Tiffany, Audrey, Lorraine, and Gloria.

Anytime my brother started beating up on me I escaped through the second-floor window, jumped onto the hood of my mother's car in the driveway, and ran as fast as I could to my refuge a few blocks away.

When Mom wasn't around I'd hang out with my cousins. They were mad cool. I used to love going to their house.

Tall-Boy-Jack was my main man. He was a year older than me and an excellent gymnast. There wasn't much that Tall Boy couldn't do when it came to gymnastics. He was the best in the neighborhood at backflips and cartwheels.

Tall Boy and I had gone to Samuel High School to swim over the summer. I didn't know how, but Tall Boy was an expert at that as well. He could do backflips and somersaults off of the diving board like a professional Olympian.

I went into the water, but steered clear of the deep end. When Tall Boy realized I couldn't swim, he called me poolside at the deep end. My dumb ass went to him, thinking nothing of it. Tall Boy pretended that he had something to tell me, but once I reached him, he pushed me into the deep end of the pool.

I screamed, "I can't swim!"

"Swim, Rock Hard, or you're gonna die!" Tall Boy yelled back.

Arms flailing all over the place, I tried to stay afloat, but panic seemed to draw me under. Tall Boy jumped into the water and calmed me down, and then patiently taught me how to tread water to the edge of the pool. He had done to me what his father, Lyle, had done to him and the rest of my cousins. I learned to swim in the deep end of the pool because of his unorthodox teaching methods. By the time we left, I was no longer afraid of drowning.

My cousin was a good-looking young man who was pretty popular with the ladies. We both attended Middle School, near Metropolitan Avenue. There were a lot of roughnecks from my neighborhood that attended the school, so every kid had to have a good knuckle game. There was always a chance that somebody was going to try you sooner or later.

Since I had a big family I always had someone to protect me, and my cousins now living in the neighborhood just made things better. Tall Boy was more of a brother to me than a cousin, and he was very overprotective of me. He was famous for his curly hair, while most people admired me for my Baxter.

We both went to school in the latest fashions—always well dressed for kids our age. I'm talking about the mock neck shirts and Lee jeans era. They went just right with a pair of leather and suede British walkers, some Bally's or Clark shoes. In winter, my cousin and I kept up with the style by sporting what we called an *Applejack Kangol* hat, with fresh leather Bombers from Delancey Street.

Tall Boy and I hung out in school, and afterward, I spent most of my time at his house. There was always something crazy funny going on when I was there. For instance, whenever someone was about to put their favorite food into the refrigerator, they announced, *"I'm spitting on my food!"* Which they did, while we watched. Then, they'd store it in the fridge. Of course, nobody else touched it after that. I used to die laughing. Oh my God. That was so funny to me because nothing like that ever went on at my house.

Tall Boy used to like to play around a lot, and had this one thing he did that always pissed me off. Whenever we'd be walking, he would slow down a step in order to get behind me, and then sweep my left leg into my right one, making me trip. No matter how many times he caught me before I fell it still annoyed me.

My cousin was also superstitious. He didn't want us splitting apart to walk around a light pole. If he and I were walking together and I stepped off the sidewalk to go around a light pole, he made me say "Bread and Butter." That way we wouldn't break our bond.

"Hardhead make a soft ass" is what our elders used to say right before one of us would be heading for trouble. I say that because Tall Boy and I stayed in a jam. There was one thing in particular that we did often that kept me in hot water. We would ride our pedal bikes over to my other cousin Bry's (of all people)—and my mother hated it.

I risked getting into trouble because Tall Boy and I enjoyed hanging out at Bry's and playing around with the DJ equipment. This was in the early 80's when hip-hop music was swiftly growing in popularity. This was the DJ and rap era. My cousin would rap and I would DJ. That's all we did when we went to Bry's place—listen to music, spit some rhymes, and DJ until we were tired. We loved every minute of it.

Tall Boy and I rode everywhere on our pedal bikes. When we weren't at Bry's, you could find us at Rome Park. It was one of the largest parks in the Bronx, with a wooded area and trails, ideal for a couple of kids on dirt bikes. We passed many a day at the park, zooming up the dirt hill trails, Bunny Hopping through the air. Tall Boy was much better at it than me. He was fearless. He was like a black Evil Knievel, daring like no other.

Tall Boy and I were *this close*. I enjoyed hanging with him every minute of every day—until his dare-devil attitude propelled him into a tragedy that changed all of our lives.

5

Late Night Visit

Since I had such a large family, we were blessed to have plenty of friends. We helped many people with just about anything they needed. For years, we didn't even lock our doors. People moved through our house all day and night as if it was Grand Central Station. On weekends, we had all different nationalities from our neighborhood coming into and going out of our home.

I began to compare all of the stories about the ghosts surrounding my baby crib and visiting us, with the many different people that stopped by to check on us. It was great to experience that kind of community love, and it was that way because my mother was cool with everybody. If anyone was going through some tough times and needed a place to stay, Mom found a spot in our home for them until they got back on their feet.

By the time I was fourteen, Noah, Tall Boy's older brother, had three small motorcycles. One of them was a black and white Yamaha MX 80, one was a black and yellow Yamaha YZ 80, and the third was a red and black GT 80. They were all made in 1982. Noah used to let Tall Boy and me hold the MX 80 from time to time, and we'd occasionally take it for a spin to Rome Park.

In the summer of 1982, Tall Boy and I rode the trails in Rome Park on the MX 80, just like we used to do on our pedal bikes. I was fourteen and Tall Boy was fifteen. It was a gorgeous summer day with sweet breezes moving through the trees and plenty of other visitors along the trails.

Tall Boy decided to do some daredevil stunts on a hilly trail where there was nobody else around. He sped up the steep hill at full speed, and sailed through the air like a professional stuntman. I, on the other hand, was afraid to try any such thing.

When it was my turn I proceeded cautiously. Too slowly, in fact, because as I reached the top of the steep hill the bike cut off on me, and I went tumbling down. Once I hit the bottom of the hill, the bike landed on me, and pinned me down. It was lying across my right leg, with the exhaust pipe burning into my calf, and baby it was cooking! My cousin rushed over and lifted the bike off of me, but my flesh had stuck to the exhaust pipe like cheese burned into a frying pan. I screamed like a sissy.

"Come on Rock Hard! Let's get you home!" Tall Boy said, while helping me up off the ground.

During the ride back, I held onto the two metal bars underneath the seat on both sides. Tall Boy hit a bump while riding across a grass field and almost catapulted me off the back of the bike. He was trying to get me home as fast as possible. When we rode into our neighborhood, he made a wild U-turn on Clear Avenue, causing my left knee to collide with the rear bumper of a parked car.

I was hurting badly by the time I got to Aunt Cheryl's house, and in such excruciating pain that I couldn't scream anymore. When she saw me and Tall Boy she freaked out. While he spoke a mile a minute trying to get her to help me she screamed, "Boy, why didn't you take Rock Hard to his house?!"

"I wasn't thinking," Tall Boy replied as Aunt Cheryl examined my leg.

She was right. My house was closer. After she checked my injuries, she realized that they were not that bad at all. As for me, I decided that wild horses wouldn't get me back on a bike anytime soon. I was done with bikes for a while.

But, Tall Boy kept on riding. His brother and all of his friends had motorbikes. A friend of my older cousin, Noah, had a motorbike called an MB 5. It was bigger and faster than we were used to riding. A lot of people had respect for Noah, so when his younger brother, Tall Boy, asked one of his friends for a ride on their bike it was no problem.

The following summer a couple of friends and I were at Rome Park riding the trails on our pedal bikes. Out of nowhere, Tall Boy and another friend, Pillow Talk, rolled out onto the trails. Tall Boy was riding the borrowed MB 5, and Pillow Talk was on the back. We hung out for a while taking turns riding the MB 5 until my cousin decided to call it a day and return the bike to its owner. The rest of us called it a day, as well.

Of course, Tall Boy and Pillow Talk made it back to our neighborhood before we did. When I got home, my mother was looking out her bedroom window, shouting to me to come inside. I didn't know exactly what Mom had called me in for because once I reached the top of the stairs I heard someone banging frantically on the front door and raced back down the stairs to answer it.

Carl, a friend of my cousin, sped right past me and flew straight upstairs, sobbing. Confused, I followed him. As we reached my mother's bedroom, Carl hysterically blurted out, "Tall Boy got hit by a car on the motorcycle!"

My mother hopped off her bed and got dressed. She and I jumped into her car and headed to General Hospital in Bowery, Bronx. We were the first to arrive at the hospital. When we reached the ER, we were given the most horrible news of our lives—Tall Boy had died on arrival.

We learned that he had been riding along Part Of Me Ave. with Pillow Talk on the back of the bike when a car sped out from behind them and raced up on the right. The car passed them then made a sudden left turn. It happened so quickly that as soon as the car swerved left, Tall Boy slammed directly into the middle of it. He and Pillow Talk flew off of the motorcycle. Tall Boy's ribs had broken and ripped into his heart.

The doctors said that he hadn't felt a thing, and had died instantly. Pillow Talk was another story. He was thrown into the air above the power lines, and was in a coma for quite some time.

I can't recall in this lifetime ever feeling the amount of pain that I did at that moment. I cried like a baby.

His sisters, Gloria and Audrey, soon arrived with Aunt Cheryl. When they let us see his body they completely lost it in the ER. Tall Boy's sisters sobbed over him and hugged his broken body. Auntie Cheryl was in total shock, and in the worst pain imaginable. There is nothing worse than a parent losing a child.

Mom and I eventually left the hospital to take that long, somber drive home. I turned on the car radio to listen to some music hoping to escape the reality of my best friend's death, but the song that piped into the car burned itself forever into my memory — "Maniac" by Michael Sembello.

> *"It can cut you like a knife, if the gift becomes the fire*
> *On the wire between will and what will be..."*

How sadly appropriate.

As we drove up the driveway, there was a crowd of people gathering in front of our house. Bad news travelled fast. A lot of our friends from the neighborhood were there speaking of sorrow. On this particular day, it flowed like water. There was a huge gathering at my Auntie's house as well. Lots of friends and family came by to mourn the loss of my cousin, Jack Holiday.

Later that night, when the calm finally settled over the storm, Annabell sat on her bed reading the Bible as usual. She was used to her household getting visitors at all hours, so hearing the front door late at night wasn't uncommon. What was odd about this particular evening was that after the door opened and closed she heard someone's footsteps climbing the wooden stairs.

She left her bed to glance out into the hallway, but discovered that there was nobody accompanying the sound of these footfalls. There was a brief pause, and then the steps continued quickly towards her bedroom before entering the room, and approaching the edge of her bed.

She heard Jack Holiday's voice ask "Aunt Annabell, why were Gloria and Audrey crying over me in the hospital?"

"Tall Boy," she answered, "you died in a motorcycle accident. You're no longer with us."

The sound of Jack's footsteps immediately left her room, descended the stairs, and went out the front door. Devastated, Annabell crumbled into tears. My younger brother, Curtis, overheard our mother speaking to Tall Boy, but hadn't heard Tall Boy speak to her, nor did he hear the sound of his ghostly footsteps.

I was sad for a good while, and in a lot of pain. I had lost a brother, a cousin, a protector, and my best friend. My life wasn't the same. Everywhere I went memories of Tall Boy followed.

On more than one occasion, while walking down Voice St. in either direction, someone would trip me from behind, the same way Tall Boy used to do. I'd glance around to find nobody there. At least—nobody that I could *see.*

After that sad year ended, Mr. and Mrs. Miller, who lived across the street from us, had their grandson move in with them. He was about my age, and his name was Rha Rha, which meant something in Arabic. Rha Rha had hazel-brown eyes that matched his brown complexion, and walked with a little bop because he was bow-legged. He had moved from East New York, Brooklyn, and we started hanging out.

We grew pretty tight after a while. He too, had this big brother thing when it came to me. He protected me from harm, just as Tall Boy used to do. I began trying to find in him the qualities that Tall Boy used to have. Rha Rha was a bit of a roughneck. He was a pure prodigy of Brooklyn, a place with a reputation for breeding roughnecks.

On one occasion, Rha Rha asked me to go with him to Brooklyn, and I was more than willing. He had friends who still lived there and wanted me to meet them. We took the train to Livonia Ave. in East NY, and then walked a couple of blocks to Tef lon's and Killer Roy's house. They welcomed me into their home as if they had known me all of their lives. "What's good?" Tef lon, a tall, slim, light-skinned young fella spoke to me when I entered the house. "What's up?" I responded.

Killer Roy, the shorter one, said, "We heard a lot about you. Rha Rha said that you're cool."

I answered, "He said the same about the two of you."

"Are y'all hungry?" Killer Roy asked.

"Hell, yeah! I know I am." Rha Rha said.

"I can eat a little something myself." I reluctantly spoke up.

"Do you eat tuna f ish?" Tef lon asked.

Rha Rah and I both said, "Yes," at the same time, and everyone laughed.

"Okay, we're gonna need some bread, some pickle relish, a two-liter of Pepsi, and a bag of weed." Teflon stated, as he grabbed a set of keys off the table. "Come on. Let's go."

I assumed that we were headed right to a grocery store, and more than likely, a weed spot, but I was wrong. I followed them out of the house and up the street, back to Livonia Avenue. They were talking as we walked toward the train station, and I was totally thrown off when we started going up the steps as if we were going on a train ride.

I thought it was a little odd for us to have to take a train ride to a store, but once we reached the top step it immediately became clear what was going on. As an older lady came through the train station doors, Teflon grabbed her purse with two hands and tried to take it. The lady held on for dear life. Tef lon and Killer Roy dragged her down the stairs, while Rha Rha swung on her to release the purse.

Mortif ied, I watched them messing her up to steal her

purse. They busted up her legs, and punched her in the face until she let go. And then they ran. I ran with them to the weed spot, and then to the store. I was frightened out of my mind to witness something like that. I had seen this sort of violence on the news or in a movie, but that day, it was for real. I was in total shock.

Rha Rha and I still vibed a little, but I wasn't crazy about hanging out with him after that.

Our Bronx neighborhood got pretty rough after crack cocaine spread like a wildfire. It was one thing to survive the streets of New York when it came to a fistfight or protecting your neighborhood, but Rha Rha was doing things a little off the hook to create a reputation for himself and gain the twisted sort of respect that came with it.

He was doing things that really didn't make any sense. There was this one time when he was in Bowery Park on Anarchy Street and Bowery Street with some other kids from the block and seemed to lose mind. It was a nice day. There were plenty of people in the park playing basketball, chess, and enjoying the weather when Rha Rha randomly decided to beat up on a couple of stray dogs with a baseball bat.

It was like a scene from a horror movie. Rha Rha hit both dogs with blows to their heads, leaving them disoriented and in a bloody mess. He repeatedly delivered blow after blow to their bodies and heads while women and children came out of the park screaming at him to stop, and the poor dogs howled in agony.

Rha Rha got into a lot of trouble with the elders in our neighborhood because what he had done had gotten back to the block. My oldest brother, Freddie, got on him about it as well as some members of the Coleman family, who lived across the street. Tommy Coleman and Rha Rha got into a serious fistfight over the situation.

Rha Rha handled himself pretty well until Tommy caught him with a right hook to his jaw, and he went down for the count. Tommy KO'd that boy. Rha Rha carried on like that while most of us on the block believed he deserved everything he got.

A couple of weeks later, my two oldest sisters were playing with a Ouija Board, which was something I really didn't like to fool with. It was a new board game that everyone wanted to play, and of all the people that I hadn't seen in a while, guess who popped up? Rha Rha. He insisted that my sisters ask the Ouija about his father.

"What is your government name?" The spirit spoke through my sisters.

Rha Rha laughed as if it was a game, until the spirit said that something big was coming up in his life.

"Something big, like what? Ask the Ouija board what is it?" he anxiously questioned my sisters.

My sisters tried to explain that he should leave it alone, but he wouldn't. Rha Rha's face grew ugly, when my sisters f inally responded to his request.

"Your death!" the spirit responded loudly through my sister, and it frightened Rha Rha.

He grew angry at the response and flew into a rage, kicking the Ouija board off of the table. He stormed out the house, cursing and mumbling God knows what to himself.

6

Bedside Angel

I suffered from horrible asthma attacks through most of my teenage years and spent a lot of time in Amend Hospital. Sometimes, my stays lasted for weeks at a stretch. When I wasn't in school, or no one saw me for a while, my friends automatically knew that I was in the hospital.

I was a popular guy with most people back then, so I received visitors left and right. Fabiana Suarez, my girlfriend at the time, often cut school to come see me. She was my very first love on this earth. She was, and always will be, beautiful in my eyes.

Fabiana had gorgeous, slanted eyes that appeared to be Asian, which complimented her beautiful smile. She was a teenager with the body of a grown woman. Her 36-C bust and apple-bottom derrière were worthy of admiration.

She was partly Panamanian and partly Colombian, with blemish-free, caramel skin. My spirits always directed me to beautiful women of Latin origin. They set my blood on f ire.

There was another Latin girl who used to visit me when I was in the hospital. Her name was Guadalupe Mendoza, and she was one pretty Peruvian Mama. Her brother, Luis, was my friend, so I didn't cross any lines with Guadalupe, even though she and I had a thing for each other. I also left her alone during that time because of certain circumstances that she and her family were going through.

Guadalupe and her family had just suffered a devastating blow. She'd lost a sister, named Carla. I was about fifteen years of age when it happened, but sixteen when I heard the story. Guadalupe and Carla were walking up the block to catch the bus to school. At some point, they started walking in the street, and out of nowhere, a speeding car came along and struck Carla. She got caught underneath the vehicle and was dragged for more than a block before the vehicle finally stopped. I couldn't even imagine in my worst nightmare how horrific it must have been to witness something like that, and to hear the screaming that had to have gone with it.

Guadalupe had nearly lost her mind after her sister's death because they had been especially close. She was close to all of her siblings.

She and I were good friends, so whenever I was in the hospital I'd wake up to f ind her sitting at the edge of my bed with a sweet scent omitting from her. It was like seeing an angel. A smile would instantly spread across my face at the sight of her long blonde hair, styled in that early 80's, Madonna-in-her-prime hairdo. On a scale of 1 to 10, she was at the top of the charts.

Time seemed to lose its meaning when I was stuck in a

hospital bed, with an oxygen mask on my face. All I knew was that each hour felt like ten and I just wanted to get out, but that was not an option. I'm not sure what day of the week it was when Guadalupe stopped by for one of her visits. When I woke up, she was sitting on the edge of my bed with her back partially turned toward me. I simply observed her profile, while she stared out the window with the glow of the sun on her beautiful face. She finally said, "Hey baby, how are you feeling?"

I mumbled through the mask, "I'm breathing, baby." We laughed. The joke was that I was hospitalized *for having trouble breathing* because of an asthma attack. It was convenient for Guadalupe to visit me when I was laid up in the hospital, because she was seeing a therapist at Amend Hospital. She had to speak to someone to help her deal with the depression that losing her sister, so very tragically and violently, had caused. Baby girl had it hard for some time. I never knew how quickly we'd grow to really dig each other.

Be that as it may, I reminded myself that Fabiana owned my heart. It was a nice visit, as always. Right after she left, Rha Rha waltzed in with Ethan Lite, another friend of mine. Having to look at Rha Rha *or* Ethan after bathing in Guadalupe's glow for an hour was like a slap in the face that jolted me out of dreamland into reality. It was nice to see them anyway, even if Rha Rha tended to be a moron. Hospitals had a way of making me feel glad to see *anyone*.

Ethan was an average-looking dude with a well-toned physique. He held down odd jobs such as working in the A&P Supermarket and delivering pizzas after school. He had a passion for boxing. Some days he trained pretty hard at St. Pascal Baylon Church, which had a PAL within it. PAL was the Police Athletic League, an organization that was run by the New York City Police department. It was kinda like a big brother for inner city kids. They traveled to other PALs to participate in amateur boxing tournaments. It was a way of keeping inner city children out of trouble.

Ethan walked with an arrogant swagger, as most boxers did, but I thought he was an okay guy just the same. Rha Rha was his usual braggy self, but it was still a nice visit. They filled me in on what was happening in our neck of the woods, and I couldn't wait to get the hell out of that sterilized prison.

I was released a few days later. What I wanted most was to see my girl, Fabiana. That was going to be a challenge, because it was summer. When school was in it was good because she'd cut classes to come with me to my house for a little romance. During the summer it was a different situation. There was no telling when I'd see her because her parents kept a close eye on her.

I was a bit of a nocturnal creature between the ages of sixteen and eighteen, when I used to party at New York's most popular club, Latin Quarters, in Manhattan. It was a magnet for teenagers from all over New York. With that being said, sleeping was my thing in the daytime.

I couldn't see Fabiana the day I got out of the hospital, or the day after that. The weekend came around, and Mom left the city for a couple of days. I didn't think I'd get to see Fabiana *then*, either, so I snuck off to catch some sleep in my mother's bedroom. I fastened the hook lock so my siblings wouldn't be able to get in, and crashed. Sometime later, I awakened with a strange feeling of not being alone. I was lying on my side, facing the window, as the sweet scent of Guadalupe's perfume wafted up my nose. *What in the world....?*

I sat up and glanced toward her. She was asleep, lying next to me. I glanced toward the hook lock, which was now *un*locked. She had managed to jimmy it open from the outside, which would have been easy to do with a nail file. She was wearing a see-through blouse with a sexy bra, and a short miniskirt known as bubblegum jeans- pink ones at that.

I reached over and touched her shoulder. She woke up and turned towards me with eyes full of desire. Had she really been sleeping, or just pretending to be? I didn't care. I was a teenager powered by TBT, also known as Teenage Boy Testosterone overload. I leaned over with intentions of kissing her when Fabiana walked right into the bedroom.

What the hell? I was shocked. Guadalupe was shocked.

Fabiana was more shocked than either of us. I honestly hadn't thought that she would have come to visit me that day, and I most certainly had not expected to wake up and find Guadalupe lying next to me.

Fabiana stood in the doorway with her mouth hanging wide open and her hands on her hips. Guadalupe jumped up off the bed and said, "Hey Fabiana! I bet you want to be alone with him" and rushed out of the room. I didn't want to explain to my lady what that was all about because I was sexually frustrated, so before Fabiana could say anything I jumped up off the bed, grabbed her by her waist, and kissed her, which initiated a much-needed lovemaking session. Afterward, she had to leave in a hurry so her parents wouldn't come looking for her.

I thought I was off the hook.

A few days later Fabiana called. I went upstairs to my mother's bedroom where I could have some privacy. Mom, who was in the living room watching TV, hung up the other phone as I picked up my call. "Hey, baby" I said.

"What's going on with you and Guadalupe?" Fabiana immediately questioned with an attitude.

"Come on, I ain't got time for this. I told you that she is just like a little sister to me." I quickly defended the awkward situation she found me in only days earlier.

Static silence came over the wire. I knew I had some explaining to do. Then, I heard my mother bellowing from downstairs, "Swithun! Somebody's at the door for you!"

"Fabiana, hold on baby. Somebody's at the door for me," I said to my girl before laying the phone down on the bed and running downstairs.

When I got to the door, my eyes stretched wide open. Speaking of the devil- it was Guadalupe. And she was stunning. "Are you busy?"

I grinned, and quickly lied. "No not really. Bring your lovely self in here. Give me a second, I'll be right back." I ushered her inside and swiftly ran back up the stairs. By the time I reached my mother's bedroom and picked up the phone, all I heard was a dial tone. Fabiana had hung up on me.

Guadalupe and I walked to the store and grabbed some wine coolers. From there, we went to a Chinese restaurant and ordered some chicken wings and shrimp fried rice before going back to the house and enjoying each other's company. She let me kiss her but nothing more, and I was cool with it. We were intimate in a different sort of way that was oddly just as pleasing to me. We simply cuddled, talked, and watched videos on MTV.

She was like a little angel to me. I loved it when she came around to visit. She and I didn't argue. Fabiana, however, was always mad about something.

7

Death Ride

A few weeks had gone by since my release from the hospital, and I hadn't seen Rha Rha in a while. I assumed that he was doing the girlfriend thing as well. Rha Rha had been on my mind when I heard the loud beeping sound of a motorcycle horn, and someone constantly throttling it, just outside my house around 10 am.

It demanded my attention, so I went outside to see who it was. I was surprised to see Rha Rha, dressed in all black, with a helmet on his head, straddling a very nice red and white Honda CR 80. The motorcycle was in great condition. Shaking my head, I descended the steps to greet him. "What's up, bro?"

"Nothing much. Do you feel like riding?" he replied before hitting the throttle.

"Where to?"

"Let's go hit the dirt trails at Rome Park."

I jumped on the back of the motorcycle. As we rode closer to the park, I couldn't help but recall the last time I had seen Tall Boy riding in the woods.

Once we made it there, Rha Rha let me ride first since he drove us to the park. Thoughts of Tall Boy weighed heavily on my mind. I could feel his presence as I rode the trails between the trees. I became overwhelmed by his presence as I rode into the deep part of the woods.

A dismal, eerie sensation filled my gut as a strong gust of wind caused the leaves and branches to whip around uncontrollably. I began to see images of Tall Boy riding out in front of me, and I immediately hit the brakes, made a U-turn, and rode the trail back toward Rha Rha.

As I emerged from the deep end of the woods, I could see Rha Rha standing on a higher ground with the sky behind him, his head tilted back as if he were staring into the sun. I watched him from a distance, while fighting the haunting sensations still lingering in my gut. In fact, they grew stronger, as I rode up the hill to where Rha Rha stood. He continued staring up into the sky, as if he were still alone.

I put the geared bike into neutral and revved the engine a couple times, but Rha Rha wouldn't break free from whatever held him captive.

What the hell is wrong with him? I wondered before punching his arm to get his attention.

Startled, he turned to me with a strange look on his face. "Huh?"

"What the hell is wrong with you?" I finally asked.

He shook his head as if he was composing himself before responding, "Huh, what?"

"What the hell is wrong with you?" I repeated.

"Come on, let's go." was all he said.

I found it hard to believe that he was ready to leave without taking a turn riding on the trails.

We rode back to the neighborhood and Rha Rha dropped me off at my house. He still appeared a little lost. He just wasn't himself.

"Rha Rha, you alright?"

He shrugged. "I don't know."

"So, where are you going from here?"

"I don't know, Rock Hard. I don't know."

I left it alone. Rha Rha jerked the bike into gear and sped towards Metropolitan Avenue. A little confused, I tried to shake it off, and went into my house.

Later that afternoon there was a hard knock at the front door. When I answered it, I found myself thrown into a bad case of *déjà vu*.

Ethan Lite informed me that Rha Rha had been hit by a car, and that he was in bad shape. It turned out that the motorcycle Rha Rha had been riding belonged to a young man who happened to be the victim of a bike jacking committed by none other than Rha Rha himself. Ethan lived on the opposite side of Gone Ave. and Voice St., in a white mini-mansion. He was outside with some of our other crew when they all witnessed the event. Ethan quickly explained that the bike's rightful owner and his father had chased Rha Rha with their car.

Rha Rha had been speeding northbound on Voice St., away from Metropolitan Avenue, with his victim and his victim's Dad hot on his trail. He had attempted to swing a left, but was unable to see what was coming because a row of tall hedges surrounding the corner house blocked his view of the traffic speeding along Gone Avenue..

He tried to zip across Gone Ave. and fired right into a lane of oncoming traffic. A speeding car met him as if karma had it perfectly timed. Rha Rha had been tossed into the air above the power lines. On his way back down, his head struck the front of the vehicle before finally smacking into the ground.

"Yo, I never saw that much blood come from a person in my life," Ethan said, shaking his head in disbelief. "Rha Rha was just lying in a big puddle of blood with his head cracked open to the white meat for a good while before the ambulance got there. It was crazy."

"Damn, and I was just with him this morning."

"Good thing you weren't with him just now. I don't think he's gonna make it." he responded.

Ethan said that he had tried to comfort Rha Rha by talking to him. "At first he seemed coherent, but when he started to talk back he didn't make sense. Rock Hard, let's say you and I had a conversation two weeks ago, and then God forbid something tragic happened to me. You're standing over me and we are having a conversation, but as I'm lying on the ground you notice I'm talking to you in the manner I was two weeks prior, and about the same thing. That's what Rha Rha was doing."

"Get out of here. That's crazy!" I replied, still stunned by everything Ethan was telling me.

"It was like he knew we were talking but it was a conversation we had two weeks ago. You know what I mean?" Ethan asked.

"Yeah, he was out of it. That means he's in bad shape." I said.

Both of us were in disbelief as Ethan continued telling me every little detail. The ambulance had taken Rha Rha to Cohen Hospital in Fordham, Bronx, where he slipped into a coma.

I visited Rha Rha a couple of days later. His right leg, the one he had kicked the Ouija Board with, had been broken in several places and now hung in a cast with pins and screws in it. His head was wrapped in white bandages.

Rha Rha's cousin, Proff, had witnessed him come out of his coma a couple of times, and said, "He seems to be fighting something. He pulls the tubes out of himself and screams, *'Get off me! Get off me! Get off me!'* then he slips back into a coma."

This went on until Rha Rha finally passed away. I didn't know how to handle it. I'd just lost Tall Boy the summer before. I hated to think it, because I didn't feel I had the right to be anybody's judge, but I thought that Rha Rha's way of living was not living at all. He had been a friend and all, but he kind of had it coming. Rha Rha's death still traumatized me, though.

I tried numbing the harsh reality that my life was becoming with weed. It was a shame that we African-Americans and Hispanics found ourselves self-medicating with drugs as a way of dealing with tragedies like these back in those times. It was something that I noticed in our neighborhoods far too often, especially after Rha Rha's soul left his body.

***

Ethan and I started hanging pretty tight. Our neighborhood was getting worse and worse as crack addictions increased. It was becoming a war zone. People from all professions were getting hooked on it, and the police were overwhelmed to the point that they began to harass the good and the bad alike.

I couldn't count the number of times that I had turned the corner and gotten thrown up against a wall with people I didn't even know. The NYPD's 48th precinct conducted arrests with their blue steel .38 calibers thrust up against our heads. The other officers searched for what drug dealers called "work".

"Work" was a package of plastic vials in sandwich bags containing cocaine. Most of the drug dealers would have 25 vials in each bag, and each plastic vial was worth $10. So, one pack was worth $250. Normally, the worker turned in $200 and kept $50 for each pack. A worker would be given six packages at a time.

If the cops found a bag of crack they'd divide the guilt amongst whomever they had against the wall, slapping felony charges even on the good guys. To witness such an injustice at the hands of police officers had become a daily routine.

I remember seeing junkies do what we called the *"Rope a Dope"*. That was when a heroin addict was standing still in one place and began nodding out as if he was going to fall over but never did. He'd just keep coming back up and slowly nodding again, until he'd be almost bent over to his knees. A crack addict behaved differently. A person on crack was sweaty and jittery—constantly moving and talking too fast.

As a young man I often sat on my front porch thinking, *how is this possible?* None of my neighbors own the boats, airplanes, or submarines that were designed by the Russians and sold to the Colombians for the sole purpose of smuggling tons of cocaine and heroin into the United States.

Once these drugs made it into the USA, someway or another, about ninety percent of them found their way to the inner cities, affecting nothing but Blacks and Hispanics. I smelled a lab rat situation going on. At that time, I didn't have a high school diploma or any college credits, but I didn't need a degree to figure that out.

The set up was clear as day. We were not meant to survive. It was a damn shame the number of professionals I watched go down the tube. Drugs were not allowed in the White House or on our military bases, so I'd often wonder, *Why aren't our neighborhoods drug-free zones?*

I watched all of the shittery going on around me, but was unable to really do anything about it. At the same time, I had to deal with severe asthma attacks that threatened to kill me and all of the spiritual phenomena going on inside my home—ghosts, and angels, and dogs ripping through sheetrock and concrete till their paws bled...

But I thought that if this was the path that God had chosen for me, then so be it.

I continued to hang with Ethan when time allowed. He had his life, and I had mine, but we connected when we could.

Summer was running out and fall was settling in which was a good thing for me because I'd be able to see Fabiana again. although Sadly, I smelled trouble headed my way. Fabiana was a pretty girl and I knew guys would start hitting on her. It was a problem I'd had when she attended IS 747 on America Avenue in the Bronx. I couldn't count the number of fools I had fought in order to protect her.

She still had my heart. Although I had been attracted to Guadalupe, I didn't let that get out of control. And, once she realized that Fabiana was my number one and I was not about to change that, she moved on and found someone else.

As time rolled by, Fabiana and I grew even closer, but our love was a little crazy at times because she had a jealous streak. On several occasions, while she and I rode the train or bus, if she caught me glancing toward another girl she'd punch or smack me. Fabiana would set it off and I'd have to struggle to restrain her to prevent her from beating on me because I was never a woman beater. Sometimes we were thrown off before our stop, and afterwards we would go to my house and make love with the same blazing passion.

Truth be told, I was just as jealous.

8

Baby Betsy

I attended Spellmen High School on the border of Brooklyn and Bronx. My crew was a bit famous because we were from the home of Two Mic's and DJ Sky Bay-the most famous rap group in the world in the early 80's. Folks from all walks of life enjoyed their music.

SHS had a diverse crowd of students. Within the immediate vicinity of the school, the population was predominantly Irish and Italian. A few blocks further was a Hispanic neighborhood, mainly made up of Puerto Ricans. I got along with everyone because I was just that type.

I sold a little marijuana, which actually got me *out* of some trouble that was headed my way. A Puerto Rican in one of my classes named Edgar had gotten really cool with me. I had some smoke one day, and he went and bought a bottle of liquor for us to share.

We went to the park across from our high school where Edgar introduced me to a group of Hispanics. One guy was named Angel, and the other two, brothers, were Argentina and Bayamon. Argentina and Bayamon were known to be trouble, especially with the kids from Bronx.

We lit up some weed and drank Amaretto. There was a pretty good vibe between us as we spoke about our neighborhoods, which were pretty much the same when it came to the crack problem and the shootings. Since I spoke a little Spanish that I had learned from Fabiana and Guadalupe, it made us pretty tight. Knowing how to speak Spanish also got me into a little trouble with the Latin girls in the school, but that type of trouble I liked.

I was given a pass whenever there was a beef between them and the kids from Bronx because they were from West Side Bowery. None of my crew from Metropolitan Avenue had any problems with Argentina or Bayamon. Even though the kids from Metropolitan Avenue were rivals with the West Side Bowery kids, we didn't have any problems in school.

Later that week, Argentina and Bayamon got into a fight with some kids from West Side Bowery, and things got funky. The two brothers ended up stabbing four people, and it was really bad.

The following week, a heavyset kid named Rodney, from West Side Bowery, approached me in the school corridor. "Hey Swithun, can I holla at you for a second?"

I nodded. "What's good?"

"Yo, can you see if you could dead that beef between us and your boys?"

"I don't know. I'll see what I can do."

Things had gotten crazy, and although I wasn't cool

with the boys from West Side Bowery, I didn't really want to see anybody else get hurt, so I agreed.

Moments later, I ran into Edgar. "Hey Edgar, what's up?"

"What's up, bro?" Edgar responded, with a handshake.

"Let me ask you something. Do you think you can cool things down with Argentina and Bayamon?"

"It's hard to talk to them, bro. Their brains are wired wrong. But I'll see what I can do?"

"No doubt. Good-looking." I responded, before heading to the cafeteria for lunch.

When I got to the lunch room I went straight to a table filled with Latin honeys from Brooklyn who were feeling me. While I was sitting with them, I noticed another cutie two tables away who was checking me out. She smiled and beckoned me with a subtle nod of her head.

"Hey ladies, I'll be right back," I said, before stepping up to this pretty Spanish girl who was sporting a ponytail and a gorgeous smile.

"Hey love, what's good with you?" I softly spoke.

"Look, hold my bag." She passed me her book bag, stood, and marched away.

I stood there for a moment, confused. I watched her heart-shaped bottom swaying from left to right in skin-tight blue jeans, as she approached the table I had just left. She snatched my bag off of the table with authority, rolled her eyes at the Brooklyn crew, and sashayed her way back over to me.

If she was trying to get my attention she definitely had it. When she grabbed my hand, I followed her like an obedient puppy. She pulled me into a nearby staircase and introduced herself.

"Hey, my name is Nora, and I don't want you sitting at that table with them girls anymore."

I started laughing but admired her take-charge attitude. As I introduced myself, she pressed up close to me, placed her hand on my chest, and thrust her tongue into my mouth, while I was still speaking.

Ok, then. Funny how *selective justification* kicks in under pressure when you're a testosterone-powered teenager. Fabiana flashed across my mind as I grabbed Nora's ass. I rationalized what I was doing by mentally reassuring myself that Fabiana was my number one girl.

We wasted no time slipping out of school through a side door, and catching a cab to a nearby hotel, making a pit-stop along the way to get a couple wine coolers and a forty ounce of Olde English beer.

A few days later, Edgar finally got back to me on the whole Argentina and Bayamon situation. It turned out that Argentina and Bayamon had gotten arrested and were locked away on Rikers Island, best known for holding NYC's most notorious criminals. When I told Rodney it was music to his ears, and a relief to everyone in West Side Bowery.

My routine escapes from school with Nora had become our *extra-curricular activity.* I had a really good time with her that year, but Fabiana still held my heart. She was my first love. All of my extra went toward treating her to jewelry, clothing, boots, and anything else that made her happy.

Things weren't getting any better at home. Grandma Wright was still up to no good. My mother was pregnant with child number twelve. She was up late one night, sitting up on her bed reading the Bible, when my younger sister, Annabell, staggered into her room like a lost child. She appeared to be sleep-walking.

"Annabell!" My mother called out to her, to awaken her.

Annabell wobbled for a moment, before speaking. "Mommy, Grandma Wright made a deal with Satan to take my baby sister's brains out her head. But, don't worry Mommy. God is gonna send you a baby boy and he's gonna be just fine." On the final word, Annabell dropped onto the edge of my mother's bed, fast asleep.

A couple of months later, my mother gave birth to a baby girl with a hollow head. The doctors claimed to have seen a lot of strange things before, but nothing as strange as this.

Our baby sister, whom we named Betsy, lasted only thirty minutes in this world. After Mom and Jacob had a private service for her, their sadness lingered, and was compounded by the knowledge of what had caused her death.

It was a brutally cold winter that year. My bedroom had gotten moved down to the basement because my brother and I were too old to share a room anymore. The ceiling wasn't too low down there, but the beams were visible, as was the furnace. The atmosphere was somewhat dismal, since the walls were covered in brown panels. Most of the time it was warm enough, though at times it was damp, depending on the weather. It was creepy down there, what with memories of having had two dogs scratch their way through the sheetrock until their paws bled. The patch had been repaired, but still...

Shortly after I moved down, I had a dream that I never forgot. Two Indian women stood at the foot of my bed. They just stood there, while I looked around the basement to ensure that everything was in place. I focused on a jacket that was draped on the back of a chair at the table, and then the wall that had a poster of a naked girl, and then a floor lamp positioned in the corner.

I glanced back at the two women, who stared at me for a moment before they finally spoke. When they did, their two voices merged into one. "Swithun, it's in the ground. It's in the ground, Swithun, right beneath you."

I was terrified. I struggled to awaken, but finally did. I glanced around. Everything was still in place, as it had been in the dream. *Was it a dream or not?*

By the time I composed myself enough to get out of bed, I was overcome by the worse asthma attack I'd ever felt. I couldn't breathe. As I raced upstairs to tell my mother, every step I took felt like my last. I could barely knock on her door when I made it to her bedroom.

She took one look at me and jumped out of the bed, because she knew exactly what was happening. She threw on some clothes and dragged me down the stairs and into her car, then she raced to Amend Hospital.

We pulled up to the emergency entrance a few minutes later, and my mother rushed me inside. I felt as if my chest was about to explode. Mom told the Receptionist what was happening, and within minutes they had me in a wheelchair, and rushed me straight to a room. They slapped an oxygen mask over my face and administered medication through an intravenous tube to open up my airways.

"Swithun, if you don't open up, I'm going to have to open your throat up in order to put a tube in it." The doctor yelled, as I began to lose consciousness.

Thoughts of Tall Boy, Rha Rha, and the time we spent together raced through my memory, as the doctor's voice faintly echoed, "Swithun open up, big guy! Come on!"

I started to fade, as the doctor ordered his staff to start

the procedure. After preparing everything, the doctor approached me with a scalpel in his hand. All at once, I was able to breathe enough for them to avoid doing the procedure. I was scared and tearing something terrible.

A pretty brunette nurse swabbed my head with a dry towel, assuring me, "It's okay sweetie, it's okay."

After they stabilized me, my mother entered, and whispered into my ear, "Your battle is my battle."

Finally able to speak, I asked, "Ma what took them so long?"

"They were fighting over you, my child." *Them* being Angels.

By age sixteen, I had knowledge and wisdom of spiritual warfare, to some degree, mostly taught by my mom. But, this life that I was living was deeper than one could ever have imagined—myself included. I was laid up in Amend Hospital for three weeks.

Ethan Lite and his cousin, "Little L," came to visit me with some of our other crew from the neighborhood. Ethan was pretty much my running partner at the time. He was a bit saddened over me being in and out of the hospital and promised to get me a warmer coat when I got out, because he thought it might help.

After my release, I did a lot of thinking while I regained my strength. The back and forth hospital stays, and near-death experiences, caused my heart to harden, turning me into someone I had never dreamed of becoming.

Ethan Lite and I started walking the back streets of the Bronx to check out America Avenue and Bowery Estates—neighborhoods with really nice houses. Now and then we talked about how other people were living compared to our own lifestyles, what the rich had, and how they got it, what we *didn't* have, and why.

We were both fatherless, and Ethan's mother had passed away years before we met. Ethan and his Mom had been living in the projects in East Orange, New Jersey, at the time. While she had been sitting at the table in her apartment, she got hit by a stray bullet—caught in a crossfire between the New Jersey State Police and a member of the Black Panthers. To grind salt into the wound, the bullet had been fired from the gun of a New Jersey State Trooper.

I couldn't imagine the pain he was walking through life with, but if it was anything like what I was experiencing, it would explain our bond. We were two very angry young men, and one night, trouble was something we both went looking for.

On a cold December night, Ethan and I decided to go on a mission with a BB gun and sawed-off rifle. I figured with the gun not being "real" how much trouble could we get into if we got caught? We took another walk through Bowery Estates, except this time, it was at night and with bad intentions.

Two girls turned a corner, walking right towards us. Ethan said, "Get ready." Once they were close enough, He pulled out the BB gun, and yelled, "Don't move! Take off your coats!"

Terrified, they did as they were told.

"Get their bags and their coats!" Ethan ordered.

Ethan was in control of the situation, and I quickly did as he said. Ethan and I took off into the dark like the bandits we had become, with two sheepskin coats and two purses. There wasn't much in the purses but a few dollars and some makeup, which we tossed in a nearby trashcan on our way home.

It seemed like a good idea at the time, but I felt bad later on. *At least I came off with a coat,* I reassured myself. Ethan had gotten me a coat, as he had promised.

I had a coffee brown sheepskin and Ethan had a nice blue one. They f it us perfectly, and after a couple of days, we had become the talk of the town since those kind of coats were in style back then.

The mentality of our friends was such that they assumed we sold drugs to buy the coats since that was what most of the drug dealers and hustlers purchased with their money.

Times were rough, and you could tell who the drug dealers were because they strutted around in brand-new clothing, flashy jewelry, and drove nice cars. However, those who thought I had sold drugs to get my coat were dead wrong. It didn't bother me what they thought because I liked my new sheepskin. I loved the way it looked on me, and it was warm as hell.

Eventually, I changed my mind, and would become a drug dealer like most of the kids in my neighborhood.

9

The Real "G"

By then, crack cocaine had swept through like a bad storm destroying everything in its path. One night, I was walking to the store and found myself at a horrible crime scene. Mr. and Mrs. Stewart, who had given my brother and I jobs at their deli, had been robbed. There were dozens of police cars in front of the store.

Although they had yellow tape surrounding the entrance, I was able to get a good look inside. There was a large pool of blood just inside the door, next to the counter. It was chaotic. After speaking to a few people, I was relieved to discover that it wasn't the blood of Mr. or Mrs. Stewart. "God is good and all the time." I mumbled to myself, as I thanked Him for protecting them.

That was the second time that the deli had been robbed.

Apparently, three amateur stickup kids were trying to rob Mr. Stewart, who had been near the counter at the time. Instead of cooperating, Mr. Stewart grabbed the robber's gun and struggled with him in front of the counter, and it went off. The stray bullet struck one of the other would-be robbers directly in the head, and dropped him in the doorway.

Shortly afterward, Mr. Stewart purchased two small firearms—a nickel-plated .32 caliber revolver and a black .25 caliber automatic with a Pearl handle, that was just perfect for Mrs. Stewart.

Although they had purchased a couple of guns to protect themselves, the continuous and rapid deterioration of the neighborhood was too much for them to accept. They eventually decided to pack up, close the deli, and move. They made sure to wish my brother and I well before returning to the Virgin Islands.

Some time passed and I had not seen my boy, Ethan, in a little while, so I went looking for him. I ran into his cousin, "Little L," who informed me that Ethan had been locked up on Rikers Island for some other crime. It must not have been that serious, because I heard that he was out after only spending a couple weeks in jail.

At least five months passed before I actually saw him, though. In the meantime, my mother gave birth to a baby boy, named Ethan. I was so proud to have a baby brother that I spoiled him every chance I got.

As creepy as my bedroom in the basement was, my brother Amell and I turned it into a man cave. Whenever I was at home, I kept my little brother Ethan by my side at all times, listening to music broadcasting from Z100.3 FM radio station. It played the music of all cultures, but mostly soft rock, which was a genre that I enjoyed. I loved the music in the 80s, especially artists like Prince, The Revolution Band, Lenny Kravitz, and of course, Two Mic's, because they were from Metropolitan, where I lived.

Listening to music had become my way of escaping the bad things surrounding me. To create a peaceful atmosphere, I would turn the radio on, burn incense sticks of coconut oil, and drink a nice, cold, forty-ounce of Olde English beer.

Ethan Lite came for a visit while I was just chilling in the basement and babysitting my little brother, Ethan. He was excited to f ind out that he and my baby brother shared the same name.

"Big Ethan and Lil' Ethan." He continuously repeated every time he was visiting and holding my brother.

One day he visited me in my man cave while I was babysitting my little brother, and pulled out a chrome .38 special with a rubber pistol grip to show off. He was waving it around in the air when I yelled, "Yo, don't point that gun in my baby brother's direction!"

"Come on, man. If I was to hurt little Ethan, I would turn this gun on myself."

I responded, "I wouldn't want that either, so how about you just chill and put the gun away?"

Ethan Lite was a beast, but he respected my wishes and tucked the gun safely back into the waistband of his pants while I placed my little brother in his playpen.

"So, Rock Hard, have you been working out? I mean like in the gym?" Ethan asked.

"What do you think?" I replied, as I flexed my right bicep.

"Well, prove it," he said as he rushed at me, and tackled me to the floor.

This evolved into a full-blown, hard-core wrestling

match. We were getting it on for several minutes, and Ethan was talking trash the whole time.

"This is how they do you in C-74!" Ethan shouted, trying to pin me down. C-74 is a housing unit on Rikers Island for kids between the ages of sixteen and twenty, who had committed crimes and were awaiting trial. I realized that he was trying to teach me how to fight jail-style in case I ever needed it to survive.

Later that week, Ethan got picked up again by some NYPD detectives. I found out after the fact that they had put him in a lineup where the two girls whom we had robbed of their coats and purses several months prior had identified him. The detectives knew that he had had an accomplice, and had pressured Ethan hard during the interrogation to reveal who had been with him that night, but Ethan upheld the street code, and didn't snitch on me.

They also got him on some unrelated charges, but the armed robbery we had committed with the BB gun was the weight they needed to sink him. Ethan hadn't been able to convince the detectives that the gun was fake, so he took the charge by himself, like a real "G". It was a sad day when he found out that he had to serve four years in a penitentiary in upstate New York.

Ethan sat on Rikers Island for a while waiting to be transferred to the Elmira correctional facility. Before they transferred him to a state penitentiary, Luis, Barkim, a couple of my other friends and I, went to visit him. Luis drove us to the facility in his father's 1983 gray Chevy Astro van.

Rikers Island sits behind LaGuardia Airport in East Elmhurst, Queens, New York. It's a pretty large complex, and has more than one holding facility on the island. It was my first time visiting the jail that I had heard so much about.

It was a little intimidating at first glance. When we

pulled up, there was a small trailer-like booth just before a bridge with a couple of correction officers inside. They questioned where we were going, and gave us a pass to park in a nearby parking lot. We then had to take a bus across the bridge.

While crossing the bridge, I stared at the impenetrable double gates that had more than enough barbed wire around their perimeters to make the nearest neighbor sleep comfortably. Once over the bridge, we entered a building to register and put our personal items inside of lockers before getting on a bus that would take us to C-74.

Rikers Island ain't a duck walk to get in or out, I thought, when we arrived at the building with "C-74" over the doorway. We had to undergo an intensive body search before stepping through a metal detector.

After this personal violation performed by the Corrections Officers, they led us, single-file to a nearby staircase. Once we and a group of other visitors had gathered by the door, we heard a loud buzzing sound before the door opened. We all followed the Corrections Officer up the stairs and into a large, well-lit room that was furnished with small tables surrounded by chairs.

We sat at the first table next to the door. Luis, Barkim, and I engaged in small talk until the door across the room opened, and inmates began to enter. Several of them came out before my homeboy, Ethan. When he came through the door, he wore a gray jumpsuit with white sandals and socks, just like the rest of the inmates.

When I saw Ethan, he looked as if he'd eaten a horse. His arms had gotten huge from lifting weights, and he had been well-fed. Ethan gave everybody a hug before sitting down.

I said, "Damn brother! Has it been that long? You put on some serious size."

Nodding nonchalantly, he responded, "Everybody's in survival mode in here."

"Are you good?" Luis asked.

"Yeah, I'm good. I'm running the show. I'm head of the house gang so I get extra privileges like extra phone calls and staying outside my cell after lock-in...you know, things like that. Not to mention, I get to move around the building more than the rest of these cats."

Most of our crew had boxing skills, and Ethan was no exception. Although he had been in a lot of street fights, Ethan had some amateur boxing under his belt, as well. He had fought a few times in the ring, but all of us were surprised to find out that he'd had a few boxing matches while on Rikers Island.

Gazing around the visiting room, Ethan explained how PAL (Police Athletic League) had organized fights on Rikers Island from time to time. When he told us he had knocked a few cats out none of us doubted him. He was in excellent shape, a real fighting machine.

While we were visiting with Ethan, a Spanish family sitting at a table next to us—an elderly lady and a young girl that appeared to be in her late teens—were crying. The inmate they were visiting was also crying, and Ethan's eyes locked in on them as they spoke in Spanish.

"Yo, Luis. What they talkin' bout?" Ethan asked.

"Seems like the dude is complaining about how he's being treated. He wants to go home because the inmates have beaten him and taken his food and clothes." Luis translated.

Ethan locked eyes with the crying dude, grimaced, and spat, "You pussy." He turned back toward us, and we continued talking about what was going on back in Metro. That was some good entertainment for Ethan simply because time stood still in jail. All there were for my homeboy were memories. That's all he had now.

He was clearly happy to see us, but unfortunately our visit with Ethan had to come to an end. We all gave him a hug. I'm not sure about Luis or Barkim, but when he hugged me, I felt him transferring his pain of loneliness into my being. He didn't want us to go, but we had to.

The Corrections Officers made us line up along the wall. I'm sure they had their reasons, but I found it funny how they had us lined up to exit the visiting room, backward. Since we were sitting at the first visiting table next to the gate that led to the stairs, we found ourselves at the back of the line on the way out.

After a couple of Corrections Officers took their places near the stairs, they instructed us to walk around the visiting room before leaving. We were led away from the visiting area in a circular formation, while the inmates remained sitting.

Once the line of visitors made it through the gate, we followed one another down the stairs. I was the last one, and had to pass Ethan, who was still seated at the table. He had a look on his face that I had never seen before. We weren't allowed to speak to each other, or even give a high-five on the way out. After passing Ethan, I took a couple of steps down the stairs before glancing back over my shoulder at my boy, one last time. To my surprise, Ethan's eyes were watery, and a tear began to trickle down his cheek. A piece of me died in that moment. I didn't mention it to Luis or Barkim . I never spoke of it again.

Once we got off of Rikers Island, Barkim and Luis wanted to hang out, but not me. I just wanted to go home. I held in the pain that I had been harboring after witnessing Ethan's heart-breaking expression. The look on his face continuously flashed in my mind. I felt like Tall Boy had died all over again.

I often neglected the fact that my mother was "born with a veil." She had the ability to see the paranormal when she focused on something. When I got home, I went straight upstairs, looking to hold my baby brother, Ethan.

Mom was sitting up on her bed, reading the Bible. She had a way of knowing when something was off with me, so I did my best to avoid eye contact. I was afraid of what she might say, so when I entered her room, I purposely marched straight over to Ethan's crib to pick him up.

As I held him tight to my chest, she said, "What happened to your friend, Ethan, was meant for you."

Her statement caught me off guard. I lost it right then and there, and began sobbing like a child.

She went on, "What is after you will go for your friends. It will try and trick you into doing what doesn't look as bad, but yet it wants to harm you anyway it can. Your friend was a casualty of your ongoing spiritual battle. The Spirits said that Ethan's going to be okay. That he's a tough young man, and he loves you like a brother. That's why he didn't tell on you, but what you guys did was wrong. So, when the detectives were on the hunt for you two, your guardian angel stepped in and blocked what was coming after you. You, with asthma, wouldn't be able to handle jail."

I was broken inside, and had to deal with survivor's guilt. We had a couple of gatherings in Ethan's name, but the hood was never the same. Neither was I when they shipped him to a penitentiary somewhere in the mountains of upstate New York.

10

Don't Judge Me

Staying fit was our thing back then. Since Ethan was in jail, I began hanging out with his cousin, "Little L." We worked out together, lifting weights and drinking plenty of weight-gain shakes. Sometimes for recreation, we'd Smack Box with one another.

Smack Boxing is a game many of us played in the neighborhood. It was boxing, but with an open hand, and if you were caught off-guard, it could sting like hell. It could be worse than a punch if someone caught you just right. It seemed like every game we had in the neighborhood was about tough love.

When I wasn't working out or hanging out with my lady, a couple of friends and I embarked on a much more dangerous game than Smack Boxing. At night, when the drug dealers ran out of work, we'd put tan-colored soap inside the small capsules they used to sell crack cocaine. We would go up to the corner of Voice and Metropolitan Avenue, and wait for crackheads to come and purchase what they thought was crack.

We'd make several sales, and before anyone figured out what we were doing, we'd take off running, usually disappearing without a trace. We'd run like hell, laughing our butts off. It wasn't everyday that a dude could make several hundred dollars off of half a bar of soap.

My friends and I joked with one another: "Poor crackheads. Sorry for selling you guys soap, but we figured if you couldn't get high, maybe you could take a bath."

It was all shits and giggles until Wolfman, the neighborhood alligator, got wind of it. Wolfman, the "boss" who distributed packages for his gophers to move, came looking for me since I was the ringleader.

I was standing on the corner at the end of my block when he drove up in his all-black Pathfinder SUV. He stopped and waved at me to get in. I was a little hesitant but got in anyway.

"What's good, Rock Hard? I've been hearing some things about you. If you wanna get some paper I have a solution that works for both me and you. I know you live on Voice St. and it would be hard for you to do business there, but I got Bane St. and Metropolitan Avenue on lock, and the paper flow is pretty strong right now. So, rather than you getting in an unnecessary beef with the brothers at the corner of your block, just come on board with me and get this money."

"That sounds cool. But I'll get back to you on that," I told him. Our conversation was brief, and after I got out of his car I took the idea back to the rest of my crew. I kicked the thought of what I had planned with my lady, Fabiana. My girl was in love with me and would agree with me on almost everything, just as long as I was able to keep some money in my pocket.

It wasn't until I spoke with two of my closest boys—Pee Funk, from Metro, and Larry, from Graham Boulevard—that I made a decision. They were all for it. It was unanimous. Shortly after that we began working for Wolfman and making lots of cash on Bane St. It was more money than we could have possibly imagined.

We spent most of it on expensive sneakers and clothes. We sported the latest fashions like leather Pelle Pelle jackets, and of course we all kept a fresh pair of leather pants. It was our style since we were from Metro.

We were living the lives of movie stars. I took pride in attending school every day with the appearance of a rapper. I was making enough money to buy my girl and Nora anything they wanted. I would take them on shopping sprees at different times. I would buy them top-of-the-line jeans and designer leather boots, and every now and then, I'd drop a couple hundred dollars on some large gold earrings.

I had money to burn, but it came with the risk of going to jail. We had plenty of close calls. On one occasion I was hustling on Bane St. with my homeboy, Pee Funk, and we had both just gotten a $1000 pack from Wolfman to work off. For a Thursday night, things were moving pretty quickly.

Pee Funk and I agreed to stay off the corner and work in the middle of the block. We figured it would keep us out of sight of the police. Normally, somebody would give us a heads-up by shouting, *"5-0!"* if the cops were coming, but this particular night was a different story. We were so busy with customers that we didn't notice two beat cops approaching us from behind. They startled us when one of them screamed, "Halt! Police!"

Pee Funk and I started to walk away as if we didn't see or hear them. I turned and looked just as they both pulled their weapons.

"Where's your work?" I asked Pee Funk, after dropping a handful of crack vials and walking much faster.

Pee Funk started to reach into his pocket, "It's in my —"

"Don't do that! They'll shoot you!" I shouted just before we took off running. They were hot on our trail until we finally lost them, but that call was too close for comfort.

I was in the streets kind of hard at that time in my life, but no matter what I did, I never stopped believing in God. I'd grown popular and very well-respected, so people from all walks of life trusted me. It was funny because it just came from out of nowhere.

One day Justin, a friend of mine from Spark St. and Metropolitan Avenue, Mcg block, approached me with another homeboy of his. Dude was Puerto Rican, and they called him Lil' Cipriano. After introducing me to Lil' Cipriano, Justin put me in an awkward situation.

"See what you can do with this," Lil' Cipriano said, before passing me a $1000 bundle of heroin. "There's much more money in it than Cocaine."

I stared at Lil' Cipriano and our mutual friend for a moment before responding, "I'll see what I can do with it but I'm not going to handle this shit! I heard you can get addicted just by touching it."

They laughed and suggested that I get a box of latex gloves, then they left me wondering what to do with something I had no knowledge of how to go about selling. I thought about this proposition that had been forced upon me for a few hours, and then it hit me. I had an older cousin named Baby Sha who knew all about selling heroin.

I called him and he came over later that evening.

He was surprised when I showed him what had landed on my lap.

"What the fuck you doin' with this? This is way out of your league, cousin."

"Do you think you can do something with it?" I asked, already knowing the answer.

"I'll take this to my man to see what's good with it. If the quality is good, we should all be able to make some money off it."

"That's what I'm talking about," I responded, before walking him out of the house.

A couple of days had gone by since I dropped the heroin on my cousin. I was coming out of the store when I ran into Justin.

"What's good, Rock Hard? Did you have any luck with that work?"

"I'm still waiting for my peoples to finish," I said.

"Okay, that's cool."

"Hey Justin, let me ask you something. Who is that Spanish cat you brought with you the last time?"

"Oh, that's Cipriano and Peaches' son," he explained.

"Who the hell is that?"

Laughing, Justin responded, "With all the Spanish girls you deal with, you don't know who Cipriano Deleon is?"

"Nah, who is he?"

"You know who he is. I'm sure you probably heard one of his songs before. He's like the king of salsa music. You've heard of him before."

"Oh, okay. Listen, I'll get at you as soon as I hear from my people."

I still had no idea who Cipriano Deleon was, but it didn't take me long to find out that I had heard his music, and knew some people who knew his family. Later that week my cousin, Baby Sha, came around.

"Where is that young Puerto Rican boy getting that dope from?" my cousin asked.

"Why? Is something wrong?"

"Not at all, but someone will kill him for what you gave me."

"Cousin, ain't nobody fucking with him. He's with us."

Baby Sha said, "That thousand-dollar bundle you gave me was *fire*! My man made eight grand off that shit."

"Oh, word! That's cool," I shot back, excited by the amount of money that was actually made.

"Listen here, cousin, don't you get mixed up with that shit. It's nothing to play around with," he warned me.

"I won't. I already know," I assured him.

The money was good, but I had already made my mind up that it was something I didn't want to continue. So, after Baby Sha and his homeboy took their cut, I was left with $5000 to give Lil' Cipriano. I gave him the money, and he put $2000 in my pocket just before I told him I wasn't moving any more heroin.

I had a very short career in the heroin business, and since I was pretty well-respected, Lil' Cipriano gave me no static about my decision.

Soon I was back on the block of Bane St. where I still hung out, worked for Wolfman and got my paper off of crack cocaine. Things were going well until one evening around 11:00PM when I went to the corner of Bane St. and Metropolitan Avenue, and it was like a ghost town. With eyebrows raised as I scratched my head, I found it extremely odd that no one was out on a Friday.

I looked around, and after a couple of moments of trying to figure out where my crew might be, I noticed Wolfman coming up Bane St. from the direction of Away Out Avenue. He was stepping quickly with a look of concern on his face, which worried me. He had his hand in his jacket pocket when he stepped in front of me and said, "Listen Rock Hard, get off the block."

He quickly brandished half of a chrome Smith & Wesson, 9 mm pistol, and his head moved on a swivel, as if he was looking for someone.

"I'm going to serve Metropolitan Avenue tonight," he continued. I just stood there, stunned by his kill-or-be-killed mentality.

Apparently, the beef was on with a cat that we called, No-neck Freddy, and his older brother because they had robbed a couple of Wolfman's workers at gunpoint for a couple of stacks. Wolfman wanted me to get off the block, but once I flashed my burner at him, I'd made it clear that I was not going to leave him alone to handle these local stickup kids. It could've been me that they robbed, so I felt a sense of loyalty and obligation to hold my man and our block down.

Wolfman was posted up on Bane St. and Sky Ave., while I hid across the street from him on the curb between two cars. With my 38 Revolver in my hand, I was ready for anything.

It was close to midnight when things began to get really interesting. A beat cop from the 48th precinct appeared out of nowhere between Artery Street and Heart Street. He was strolling slowly toward the corner of Bane St. and

Metropolitan Ave., seemingly ill-prepared for what would happen next.

Wolfman, not noticing the beat cop, had spotted Fallon— a.k.a. *The Beast*—and popped two shots at him. He ducked between two cars and fired two shots back before he took off running. The sound of the gunshots startled me.

When I got up off the ground to help my friend, I heard the beat cop screaming into his radio, *"10- 10 shots fired! 10-10 shots fired at Bane Street and Sky Ave.!"*

I crossed the street with the gun in my hand, while Wolfman chased Fallon through the back streets of Metropolitan Avenue, between Bane, Artery, and Sky Ave. A few more shots rang out through the night air, but by the time I turned the corner, both Wolfman and Fallon were gone. The approaching sounds of police sirens sent me racing home rather than going to jail. I cut through a couple yards and jumped over a few fences to shorten the distance.

By the time I got home I was sweating bullets and out of breath. It was the first time in my life I had witnessed anything like that. The adrenaline rush was crazy—and please don't judge me, but part of me enjoyed the excitement of unknown danger.

You see, the way I figured it, after having guns placed against my head by NYPD's finest for no reason other than being a resident of my own neighborhood, I was kind of used to the cat-and-mouse game with the cops. So, at the age of sixteen, I'd already embraced who we were, and that we were not liked by law enforcement. My life was on the line every time I stepped out of my house. And it would only be a matter of time before I would f ind myself in a life-or-death situation.

11

Metro Vs. Bowery

The time came for me to make my bones in the neighborhood. A Latin gang called the Ball Busters had jumped on the scene and began terrorizing a neighborhood near my old Junior High School. Fabiana had a younger brother attending the school by then, and that concerned me.

After questioning a few people, I was informed of their whereabouts. They had a pretty rough reputation, so I considered the adds and takeaways of the situation. It didn't take long for me to realize that I wouldn't be able to recruit any of my Latin friends to get at them.

The Latin friends that I hung out with probably knew the Ball Busters members that I was after. I didn't want to risk them whispering my plan of attack to anyone who might warn them that Big Rock Hard was coming for them.

Therefore, I kept my Latino friends in the dark and only shared my plan with the Metro Boys.

Although the Metro Boys crew was strong, I felt the need to recruit a few roughnecks from Clear Avenue and Belvedere Boulevard to add a little more strength to my team. I put a few calls in and set up a meeting, which took place on Voice St., between Metropolitan Avenue and Away Out Ave.

"Little L" was my right-hand man, so he was definitely present. So was my dude, Big Roe, a tough brother I attended church with. Yes—I said *church*. Big Roe was the type of brother that was down with anything. The plan was simple and straightforward. We armed ourselves with baseball bats, golf clubs, and pretty much whatever else we could use as weapons. I suggested we leave the guns home in order to keep the noise down on the back streets of America Avenue after things got ugly.

About thirty of us went on a hunt for the so-called *Ball Busters*. As we marched through the back streets of America Avenue toward IS 747, someone driving a jet-black Mazda 626 with tinted windows rolled up on us.

"Everyone lookout for guns!" I yelled, as the car drove slowly through the midst of our crew, now walking down the center of the street. When the car came to a stop I was standing directly next to the passenger door, which popped open.

A big beast of a Puerto Rican kid with tattoos on his neck exited the vehicle with his chest puffed out and addressed us as if he was an *official gangsta. King shit.* "What the fuck y'all doin' in my neighborhood, bro?!"

His face was twisted, so I returned the expression and boldly replied, "Looking for the Ball Busters."

"Ball Busters? I'm a real Ball Buster from uptown!"

"Oh yeah?" I clapped back before glancing at my crew and sounding off, "Well, we're the mother-fuckin' Metro Boys!"

I immediately bashed his head open with a wooden club from my old bunk bed set. Blood was everywhere when he grabbed his head, staggering from the heavy blow I had just delivered.

He screamed to his friend, "Get in the car, bro! Get in the car!"

His friend was *already* in the car, when my crew moved in on them like a pack of hungry wolves. The big dude with his head split-open jumped into the passenger seat, while we went to work on the pretty black Mazda.

The driver put the car in reverse and almost hit "Little L," who had to jump up on the trunk. I smashed the window of the passenger side as the driver put the car in Drive, and tried to run us over again. The sounds of metal on metal and breaking glass resonated through the street as the driver erratically sped off. We chased the car for about a block before it turned the corner and disappeared.

After we ran up on the Ball Busters, my name started to ring bells—not only in Metropolitan, but throughout Bronx. The real players started reaching out to me, and it *felt good.* It felt good to be both loved and feared while I moved through the mean streets of Bronx.

***

My lady, Fabiana, was attending High School that year as a freshman. She was one of the most beautiful girls in her school, and for me that meant trouble. She became friends with a girl named Kim, who lived on the Bowery side.

Kim's brother, Kevin, ran with some roughnecks who

had a strong and popular drug gang. The main dude was a drug dealer named Kristan. Kristan came from a drug-dealing family. His aunt was going out with one of the Russo family, and they had a lot of clout.

I heard through the grapevine that Kevin had a thing for my girl, so I felt it necessary to ask her about it on site. "Fabiana, what the fuck is going on?"

"What are you talking about?"

"I'm hearing things about you hanging around some wannabes from around your way. You should know that I know people and I hear things, so you better come clean. Right now." I demanded.

"I don't hang out with anyone but my friend, Kim. We're friends, and I go to her house every now and then. That's it."

"So, what about her brother, Kevin?"

Fabiana's facial expression changed drastically when I mentioned Kevin's name. Her expression said, *how do you know him?*

"So, what's up with Kevin? And you better tell me everything that happened."

Fabiana started crying, and blurted out, "Nothing happened! I only watched TV with her brother on the couch one time. I swear. But he thinks I like him even though I told him I have a boyfriend."

"Is he still trying to get with you?" I asked.

"Yes, he tries to talk to me in school. And his friend, Kristan, drives a gray Jetta."

"Okay, I'll take care of it."

"Rock Hard, what are you going to do?" she questioned, wiping tears from her eyes.

"Don't worry about it. I'm going to talk to him."

When I got back to Metropolitan Avenue, I assembled

some of my crew. My homeboy, Big Roe, Till Morning—a.k.a. TM—a cat known for knocking brothers out until the next morning, and my dude, Crow, and I, had a little meeting. I explained what was going on and that I needed to put a stop to it. Their attitudes were *We are the Metro Boys. Let's do this!*

The following day we got together at around two in the afternoon and headed up to Bowery High School, where I intended to introduce myself to Kevin. By the time we got close to the school, it was approaching dismissal time. To my surprise, as we approached the front of the building, Kevin was sitting on the stairs out front with a pretty, light-skinned girl who wore a large set of Bamboo Earrings.

I intended to confront Kevin about Fabiana, but didn't get a chance because Kristan, the ringleader, walked out of the school. My attention diverted to him because I knew he was going to be a problem. His eyes locked with mine as he was coming down the steps. It must've been the look on my face, because he asked, "What's going on at my school?"

I was halfway up the steps when he made his comment, so I leapt up and punched that mother fucka right off his feet. He fell flat back on his back. Before I could throw another blow, Kevin lunged toward me. Unfortunately for him, he stepped directly into a hell of a right punch before I started beating his ass.

My boys were scuffling with a couple of other kids who had come out of the school. While I was pounding on Kevin, the girl he was talking to hit me across the face with a stick. The stinging blow to my cheekbone demanded my attention. My reflexes kicking in, I turned and punched her in the face. Her earrings flew out of her earlobes, as she tumbled down the stairs.

In my peripheral, I noticed that Kristan was running back into the school. It wasn't until security came out that we backed off of the premises. Kristan must've called his uncles, Lonnie and Surgical, because before we could get off of the block they were speeding toward us in a red Honda Prelude. They rode right past us and ended up at the school.

No one in my crew was packing a firearm, and we knew that these punks had guns. It was the only way they could win. We were stepping quickly through the back streets of America Avenue when the sound of a car speeding behind us made all of us turn and look. The red Honda Prelude was approaching fast, windows down, with an arm sticking out of the passenger window, and a gun pointed at us.

Big Roe, TM, Crow, and I only had seconds to respond, as the car sped up and two shots rang out. We quickly cut in between two houses, as they got out of the car, still popping shots at us. We split up once we got into the back of the houses, while the loud gunshots continued sounding off. It was every man for himself. I got away, but I was concerned about my boys.

By the time I made it back around the way, I learned that everyone had made it safely. From that day on it was clear that the war was on between me and most of his crew from West side Bowery.

Later that evening we had a meeting up on Metropolitan Avenue, on how we were going to retaliate. Big Roe and my boys were at the meeting along with a few others that had missed the action. We shot around a few ideas and some strategies on how to get at Kristan and his punk ass crew.

We agreed on going to war with anyone who associated with Kristan and his uncles. My whole crew had a knuckle game, but after Kristan's uncles introduced gunplay, I suggested to everyone in my crew that we stay armed at all times. Things had gotten real in the neighborhood, and it was time for us to man up or be face-down.

All of us had heard the rumors about how determined our enemies were to take us down, so we stayed on point. A couple of days later, I was at home, on the phone with Fabiana, when I heard the beeping sound of another call coming in. It was my homeboy, Little L. Before I could say hello, he screamed, "Grab your gun and meet me on the corner—*NOW!*"

I hung up without saying goodbye to my girl. I quickly got my .38 caliber revolver from underneath my mattress and ran to the corner where I met Little L.

"What's going on?" I asked, with my hand gripped tightly on the handle of my Smith and Wesson.

"I just saw Kristan's uncles, Lonnie and Surgical. They were driving up and down Metropolitan Avenue."

"These mother fuckas are pretty fuckin' bold and asking for it in a big fuckin' way!"

"That's the same thing I said to myself when I spotted them. But if they want it, then whatever," Little L responded with his hand inside his pocket, as we both scanned the street for the red Prelude. It didn't return.

That Friday night, while I was hustling on Bane St. and Metropolitan Ave. with a couple of my boys, Kristan and his uncles did a drive-by shooting on Voice St. They hit our friend, Wise, in the leg. This was too close to home. That was when I knew shit had just gotten *real* deep.

I put two and two together and figured out that someone told them I lived on Voice. They were in the neighborhood, but obviously didn't know exactly which house was mine.

Before they figured it out, *I* would hunt *them*.

On Saturdays, Fabiana attended Clever Girl's dance studio, on Throne Boulevard and Bowery Street. I went to pick her up in a cab so that I could make sure she got to the studio without incident. Her father would pick her up after her class when he got off work.

After dropping my lady off, I began walking to the bus terminal to catch a bus back to my neighborhood. When I got to the corner of Throne and Bowery Street, the light changed, signaling that I could cross. Before I could step off of the curb, I noticed Kristan, driving a gray Volkswagen Jetta, coming to a stop at the light. My eyes widened at the sight of him. I. Wanted. Blood.

I whipped out my snub nose .38 and ran up to his car. I grabbed the handle of the passenger door with my left hand, cocked the revolver with my right thumb, and pointed my gun directly at him. "I'm going to kill you!"

I was trying to pull his door open so that I could get up close and personal with him. Bad move. I'm sure he saw the devil in my eyes because he nailed the gas and sped through the red light. I stood in the street with my gun in my hand, watching him speed off. I thought to myself, *"What a stupid fucking move! I should have just fired at him instead of trying to open the door."*

Now I really had to worry about this wannabe and his family. It was a risk I continued to take just for my lady. Fabiana was my heart, and I had to make sure she made it back and forth to school without being harmed by these idiots.

On many different occasions Kristan's uncles had been spotted on Metropolitan Avenue, and each time I would get a call from one of my boys. By the time I snatched the ratchet from under the mattress and made it to the Avenue, they'd be gone. My crew and I would discuss how bold these fools were becoming, and we were anxious to catch them slipping before they caught one of us. We eventually decided to go on the hunt for them, but didn't really know what part of West side Bowery they lived in.

The summer rolled around, and one particular night on Anarchy St. in Bowery Park, there was a jam going on. DJ Sky Bay was the DJ and Mad Rapper was on the microphone, which was kind of odd to me. Bay was from Metropolitan Avenue and Mad Rapper was from Graham Boulevard, not to mention I was used to seeing DJ Sky Bay with Two Mic's.

Anyway, to our surprise, Kristan's uncles, Lonnie and Surgical, were in Bowery Park. I was there with a large group of the Metro Boys and we shadowed them in the park the entire evening. As the night went on, the party people came out and overcrowded the park. I believe that was when Lonnie's and Surgical's sixth sense kicked in.

Lonnie turned around and looked directly at me and about sixteen other members of the Metro Boys. Lonnie, Surgical, and their friends started to make their way to the main gate entrance in the park. We were close behind. I raised both of my arms to stop my crew from following them because I didn't want them to start shooting at us in the park. That way, neither our people, nor anybody in the park who had nothing to do with our beef, would get hit.

Once Lonnie and Surgical made it out of the park, they hurried to the left towards a running car. Surgical was opening the door on the passenger side as my whole crew maneuvered out of the park and into the street. Both of them were safely inside of a rusty, navy-blue Oldsmobile, but tension was in the air.

I had to give it to these two motherfuckas, because they were as bold as they came. As the car began to back up towards us, I spotted a gun with a long barrel sticking out of the passenger's window, and knew that I had to act quickly. I raised my revolver and fired the first shot. When they returned f ire, it triggered everyone in my crew to open f ire on the car.

So many guns blazing at the same time made the moment feel like something straight out of a movie. It was a proud moment for me to see my neighborhood stick together as a united force. Dozens of gunshots pierced through the air and it was loud as hell because we were underneath a train trestle. The gunshots were so thunderous that they echoed throughout the entire neighborhood.

A fog of smoke overwhelmed the street and police sirens could be heard in the distance. We decided to clear out. Those of us who were on foot used the train tracks as a means of escape because they ran parallel to Metropolitan Avenue. Once upon the tracks we raced down them until we reached our block.

Oh my God, did I have a reputation after this gun battle. Everyone in the neighborhood knew my name.

The respect you received when you defended your neighborhood was wonderful. Who would ever have guessed that Steven Mic's Williams, from the rap group Two Mic's, wanted me and one of my right-hand men to keep him posted on the progress of the war between my Metro Boys and Kristan's family.

Apparently, the generation before mine knew exactly what was going on, and the elders in our neighborhood were pleased with what was taking place. They had experienced the same thing with West side Bowery years before us. Metro and Bowery had been feuding for decades. The only difference between us and the generations that came before us was that we were heavily involved in gunplay.

12

Spirits At Work

Every time I turned around it was getting worse and worse with Kristan and his bullshit. On one occasion, after I walked Fabiana to the Greenline bus, on Smith M, Victoria Boulevard and Bowery Street, I had another run in with this Bowery boy. Once my lady was safely on the bus, I walked across Bowery Street to the opposite side. I was walking toward Storm St. so that I could catch the BX2 bus back to Metropolitan Avenue. While approaching Storm St. a gray Jetta pulled up to the curb, the doors swung open, and Kristan and a wannabe gangsta named Blue-Eyed Bully, rushed out. As they approached me, I placed my hand inside my coat pocket to grab my gun. I had my hand gripped tightly around the handle and my finger on the trigger when Blue-Eyed Bully shouted, "Yo! Let me talk to you for a minute!"

He and Kristan were still advancing toward me when I shouted, "Back the fuck up!" They ignored me, and once they were in my space, I pulled out my .38 and aimed it at Blue-Eyed Bully's face. "Back up off of me!" I yelled one more time, but they continued to play my bluff, so I pulled the hammer back on my revolver.

Blue-Eyed Bully crunched up like I'd already shot him in the chest.

A woman standing nearby saw what was taking place, and screamed at the top of her lungs, "He's got a gun!"

I glanced in her direction. Out of the corner of my eye I saw two beat cops across the street. They were looking around to see what had caused the commotion as Kristan and Blue-Eyed Bully dashed back to their car.

That distraction had saved both of their lives. I took off running down Storm St. towards America Avenue with the burner still in my hand. It was not until I reached the street before America Avenue and made a right turn toward the bus terminal, that I finally tucked the gun back into my jacket. I was stepping quickly, breathing hard, and sweating profusely.

When I made it to Storm St. there were two more uniformed beat-walking cops from the 48th St. Precinct poised at the terminal entrance. I slowed down and did my best to regain my composure. I was sweating like a crack addict as I nervously passed the two police officers who were talking to each other and paying me no attention.

I got past them and made my way to the bus just in time to see that the driver had just closed the doors. I knocked frantically as he put it in reverse. The bus driver looked at me and I gave him the saddest looking puppy face ever.

In the glass door's reflection, I saw desperation all over my face while I prayed he'd let me in before I found myself in jail. God had mercy on me that day because the door opened, and the bus driver let me get on. The whole time I was having visions of the beat cops in front of the bus terminal hearing about the situation I'd just run from broadcasting over their radios, patting me down, and locking me up. Instead, I'd escaped again. I thanked the Almighty God during the entire bus ride.

When I made it home safe and sound, my mother wasn't looking too good and asked me to ride with her to the hospital. While we were riding, I glanced over at her and when I saw her face, it wasn't my Mom. That scared me to death.

By the time we arrived at Amend Hospital, she had grown too weak to get out of the car without some assistance. Mom's health was all out of whack. I raced into the hospital, and security came out to the car with a wheelchair and rushed her inside. She was having an asthma attack that wouldn't quit, amongst other things that had her fading in and out of consciousness.

The doctors didn't know what the hell was going on with her. Her life was slipping away with each breath she took.

"Get…me…a…Priest…" she gasped.

Someone called a Priest from a nearby Chapel who hurried over. When he walked into her room, he stepped close to her bedside, and produced a Bible. The doctor and nurses witnessed something they had never seen before. My mother's life instantly poured back into her, as the Priest began to read Scriptures.

Her breathing returned to normal. The Priest leaned in closer, looked into her eyes, and smiled. She returned his smile, as the Priest stated assuredly, "You know who to call on."

One of the nurses fainted, and the doctor slammed back against the wall in total shock. They had just witnessed a spiritual healing right before their eyes. It was a testimony that spiritual warfare could even be overwhelming for those who were unaware of it.

My frustration towards my witch of a grandmother escalated. It was a phenomenon that was unexplainable, and therefore, inadmissible in a modern court of law, so she could continue casting her spells until Hell froze over and never be held accountable.

My mother and I were aware of it as it was happening, not that my siblings didn't have gifts of their own. For example, my younger brother, Curtis, would see two spirits from time to time who would give him numbers for my mother to play when we were short of money. During those times in the old neighborhood we had what you would call a Number Hole. It was an illegal location where we were able to place bets to win money. In times of need, the spirits would come through to help my mother provide for her children.

My mother was aware that I had a few girlfriends who were crazy about me, and that I bought them nice things with the money I earned from the block. Mom didn't approve of my activities, so when I tried to give her money she refused to accept it. *"Blood Money,"* was what she called it.

Eventually, to honor my mother, I had to find a way to earn money in an honest way. I needed to change anyway because I was also doing terrible in school. Once a Dean caught me cutting class in the back staircase with my lips locked onto some Latin honey's. I was always a sucker for

Spanish women. And on too many occasions I was busted by Spellman's famous Dean Bukowski.

Dean Bukowski knew me personally and had suspended me a couple of times without telling my mother. But, on one occasion, he had kicked me out of school and I had to tell my mother in order for me to get back in. She went off like a bomb! She had this incredible way of making a person feel as small as an ant. She told me off in the worst way and in just about every language possible.

My mother, Annabell E. Wright, being a tough Brooklyn woman, drove me back up to school the following day. She made me apologize to Dean Bukowski for my bad behavior and promise that it would never happen again. I was embarrassed when he told her about my extra-curricular activities in the back staircase with a pretty Latina. Mom dredged another promise out of me— that I'd be attending school for the sole purpose of getting an education. She wasn't having any more of my nonsense, and I knew she meant business.

My biggest worry was my lady, Fabiana, getting back and forth to school by herself. With the beef I had going on with West side Bowery, it was a little too much for me to leave her hanging. Being a teenager in love could really hit home at times.

After some time had passed, Fabiana began receiving threats from girls and the Bowery Boys. She informed me that they wanted to jump her after school, so I asked some of my friends to shadow her for me to make sure things never got out of hand. She was told they were going to harm her because Kristan and his crew couldn't get at me. Most of the kids from Bowery feared me because I was known to be armed, and not afraid to pull the trigger, but the situation began to escalate and get totally out of control.

A few weeks had gone by since I promised not to cut school. I made a decision to start showing my face around my lady in her school again in order to discourage any negative actions toward her. On the day that I cut class to go up to Bowery High School to walk my lady and her brother to their bus stop, I was met with the surprise of a lifetime. After we left school property, we decided to go to Bowery Plaza Mall on Storm St., and headed in that direction.

We made it to Stonewall Ave. and Storm St., where we turned left. In front of the Plaza were more than thirty of West side Bowery's most notorious members. One of them was Blind Monkey, and he had it out for me because he and Kristan were pretty tight. I wasn't carrying my gun, and it was too late to run and hide because I saw them, and they saw me.

I decided to use psychology on them. I knew that they assumed I was armed, so I put my right hand into my empty pocket and walked through their midst, holding Fabiana's hand and showing no fear. Every one of them stopped what they were doing to glare at me. I glared back without flinching. Not one of them moved.

As we strolled down Storm St. towards Bowery Street, I said to Fabiana, "Look back and tell me if they're coming." As we crossed the street to the opposite side of Bowery Street, she answered, "No."

"Look, walk a little faster," I instructed her and her brother, as we stepped quickly towards Smith M, Victoria Boulevard. I repeated, "Fabiana, look back and see if they're coming."

This time she glanced backward, and her expression screamed *danger!* She answered, "They're coming!"

I turned around, still bluffing as if I was armed, and it

seemed to me that the crowd had grown from thirty to sixty. Without thinking, I yelled, "You mother fuckers want me!"

I was stalling so that my lady and her brother could get clear of the mob. I stepped into the middle of the street on Bowery Street, as Fabiana and her brother went in the opposite direction. I kept my hand in my pocket, continuing the charade as they moved to the opposite side of the street, sizing me up for the kill.

"You mother fuckers want me? Then come and get me, you bastards!" I screamed.

I took off running back towards Storm St., knowing they'd come after me instead of going after my girl and her brother. While I was in f light one of the Bowery Boys members was on me. I could almost feel his breath on the back of my neck.

I stopped in mid-flight and turned around with a comb in my hand. The dude stopped as if I had a gun. He ducked between two cars as if his life was on the line. Everyone else burst into f its of laughter. I mean, deep belly laughs.

I seized the opportunity to slip into VIM's clothing store at the corner of Bowery Street and Storm St. Inside my head, I could hear Ethan Lite's voice, *"Whenever you're fighting a crowd, play the wall and throw all the kicks, punches, and headbutts you can."*

I made my way to the back of the store to put my back up against the wall, with a mob from West side Bowery close behind. They poured in like a heavy rainstorm, filling up the half-empty store. I continued to bluff them as if I wasn't afraid.

The first one that came into the store was a heavyset guy, so I cracked a joke on him, "I take it you need a breathing treatment, huh Big guy?"

The workers in the store started to laugh as if there was no more work to do. Even his crew laughed. With my back up against the wall, I was prepared to give it to whoever came close to me.

When Blind Monkey made his way into the store, his crew parted like the Red Sea. As he started to walk towards me, I shouted, "Blind! I know where you live, Blind!"

His expression shifted to, *how in the hell does he know me?*

"Where do you know me from?"

"You be with Ronnie Joe, Timmy Joe, and my brother, Amell."

"Amell is your *brother?*" He asked, as he lifted his arm to stop his crew from further encroachment. "Are you sure we're talkin' bout the same Amell?"

Blind was thrown a bit, because my brother had a very light complexion and hazel eyes, and I was the complete opposite, a dark-skinned fella. Nevertheless, it worked in my favor, because Blind was willing to squash the beef on the strength of my brother.

I was still in distrust mode when a middle-aged black gentleman, purchasing something in the store, came to my aid like an angel sent to protect me. He'd witnessed the whole confrontation. As I was reluctantly exiting the store, he grabbed my shoulder and stopped me. "Don't go out there. Wait for me," he said before turning and paying for his items.

He walked outside with me and then marched over to two beat cops where he pulled out a badge and told the officers what was going on. They responded by cooling the fire under Blind and his crew's butts. As it turned out, the gentleman was an off-duty police officer from the 48th St.

Precinct. He went one step further and offered to walk me
to the bus terminal, and then he wandered off.

Blind Monkey and a couple of his crew had followed
us to the bus. When I was alone, Blind approached me
peacefully. He said we wouldn't have anymore beef from
that day on. I really didn't trust him, but he seemed like he
really meant it.

When I made it back to the neighborhood I found out
that my brother, Amell, had had an encounter with Kristan
on Metropolitan Avenue. As the story went, Amell and
Timmy Joe were hanging out on the corner of Ocean St.
and Metropolitan Avenue when out of nowhere Kristan
walked to the corner shouting, "Metro Boys, Metro Boys!"

Timmy Joe said to Kristan, "What's your fuckin'
problem?"

Timmy was from the Bowery, and he and Kristan knew
each other well.

"I'm talking to the light skin brother right here. He be
with Rock Hard and them."

"Why wouldn't he be? That's his mother fuckin'
brother."

"Rock Hard brother?" Kristan responded, staring at
Amell.

Amell reached toward his back pocket and pulled out
his 380 pistol, but kept it behind his back with his finger on
the trigger. "What's it to you, mother fucka!"

Kristan's skinny punk ass said, "Well, tell Rock Hard I
was around."

I was furious when I got wind that Kristan had been
two blocks from my house, and even more so for him
confronting my younger brother about being a Metro Boys
member. It bothered me that Kristan had the nerve to come

to Metropolitan Avenue at all. Why was he trying so hard to get hurt?

Kristan kept on walking along the edge of the lion's den— That's exactly what my neighborhood was to him, considering how many people wanted to smash his face and eat him alive. We all wanted a piece of him, but nobody wanted that more than I, and Lord knew I could not wait for that day to come.

13

Caught Slipping

It wasn't long before I reverted back to skipping school. If I wasn't in the hospital recovering from asthma attacks, I was cutting classes to be with my girlfriend to satisfy both of our sexual appetites.

One day while I *was* at school, Chipped Tooth Juan, a cool Dominican dude from Brooklyn, and I were rolling dice in the lunchroom—we played C-Lo, a game that required three die. Surrounded by onlookers, we played with about seven hundred dollars on the floor. We were deep in the zone, totally focused on the game, and completely oblivious of the fact that Dean Bukowski had entered the lunchroom.

"Wright! You're out of here!"

All eyes snapped toward me.

Oh, shit.

I was officially kicked out of school in the 10th grade. When I got home my mother screamed on me like nothing I'd ever heard, which made me feel like the smallest person on earth. There would be no more chances and we both knew it. I was out of school, for good.

To make matters worse, shortly after that I got robbed of twenty-five hundred dollars in cash, three thousand dollars in crack cocaine, and my snub nose .38 caliber. It was as if God wanted to end my hustling career, and it worked.

Not long after taking such a heavy loss, a neighbor told me how to get a job at Speedway Race Track. It was located on Jerusalem Turnpike with part of it in Bronx and part in Brooklyn County. There was an entrance off of Jerusalem Turnpike that led to the backstretch where the horses were held in stables. I was told that it was the perfect place to hang out because when the trainers entered they'd hire workers if they needed help.

I got lucky the first day. An assistant trainer named Sammy asked me if I was looking for a job. I replied, "Yes, Sir!" He told me to get into his car, and I did with a smile.

While driving to the backstretch, Mr. Sammy, a small Caucasian man with glasses and a balding head, explained what the job entailed. I was given the position of "Hot Walker". A Hot Walker was pretty much at the bottom of the pecking order.

Soon, I was off to work. When the Exercise Riders returned from the track to the barn in the Courtyard, a Groomer was waiting for the horses so he could bathe them. After the horses were bathed, the Hot Walker walked them around a shed row inside the barn for forty-five minutes. At the same time, the Groomer cleaned out the stall and put down new bedding—a type of straw hay for the horses to lie on. A typical day lasted six hours.

I walked at least five horses seven days a week. Sometimes, I'd work a race in the afternoon to make extra money. When working with a race, I walked the horse after its run. If the horse won the race, it had to be led to a special barn to be walked until it urinated. During this process, blood samples were taken from the horse to determine if the trainers had administered any performance drugs. Once that was done, I walked the horse back to the barn, and gave it one or two turns through the shed row until the groomer was done preparing the stall.

Since I was a fast learner, I got the hang of the profession in no time. What I learned about myself at sixteen was that I enjoyed being challenged, and helping to train thoroughbred horses was forever more challenging. I took pleasure in being a winner as well as being a part of a winning team. I quickly came to realize that I was employed at one of the richest horse training barns in Speedway Race Track, and it was one lucky ass racing stable.

I had stumbled upon greatness and didn't even know it. Racing stable, Barn #52, was also one of the most attractive stables, by far. It was a pretty, dark green and white stable, surrounded by white ranch-style fencing. It sat on about four beautifully landscaped acres. J. Clinton's stable had the fullest and darkest green grass, matching the color of the stable. Concrete flowerpots overflowing with bright, colorful f lowers, sat at every corner of the landscape.

I had the pleasure of walking some of the most expensive horses in the world at Barn #52 such as Fast Girl, the daughter of the world's famous Secretariat, as well as With

The Wind He Blows, Stall Them, and many more. Each horse trained by J. Clinton Hawthorne was worth millions.

I really loved working there. My boss, Mr. Sammy, took a liking to me because I followed orders pretty well, and I was fond of working with the horses. Hawthorne Jr., the only son of J. Clinton Hawthorne, was a nice person to talk to every now and then, and nice to work with.

J. Clinton Hawthorne Jr. and Mr. Sammy had one thing in common— They both trusted me when it came to their food. I ran to the store for them regularly. Mr. Sammy's order changed somewhat, but J. Clinton Hawthorne Jr. always wanted the same thing for the three years that I worked there—a roast beef sandwich with Swiss cheese, butter, and mayonnaise.

I felt important working. I'd come home smelling like horses, but my mother was actually proud of me. After all, Jacob Davis, the man of her life, was a horseman.

Working hard didn't completely disconnect me from my *other* life. Once in a blue moon, I still hung out with my homies, and at other times, with my Latin crew— Luis Mendoza, Joe, and the ever-gorgeous Puerto Rican goddess, Maribel Martinez. Between my Latin crew and my lady, I learned to dance to salsa music and I picked up some Spanish. I was deeply immersed in the Latin culture— the food, ladies, language, and music. On weekend nights, Fabiana and I caught a train and a bus to Manhattan, to New York's famous Roseland Ballroom, to get in some dancing. Whenever I wasn't with Fabiana I would go to Manhattan with my Spanish crew.

One night while standing with Maribel Martinez and my Spanish crew in line outside a club named *Latin Quarters* I spotted one of the Bowery Boys members. He had been with Blind Monkey and most of West Bowery on the day I got chased down Bowery Street. My radar sounded off, but I was out for a night of fun, and just prayed for the best. He was with another one of his crew members. They looked pretty sharp in their fur coats, thick gold rope chains, and large medallions. Rap star wannabes. I kept a close watch on them.

Once inside the Quarters, I noticed them chilling in the lounge area, not too far from where Maribel and I were sitting. We made brief eye contact, but nothing serious. Moments later, we bumped heads again at the bar while I was getting drinks. Again, we made eye contact, and to my surprise, one of them offered a handshake. I gave him a long hard look before agreeing, at which time, we laughed. Thankfully, the tension dissolved.

His name was Alfonso Sancho. He and his partner, Floyd, turned out to be really cool dudes. We started hanging out together in both my neighborhood and theirs. They had my back, even in my situation with the West side Bowery crew, and I had theirs. My friendship with them even cooled things down to some degree with most of Kristan's crew.

I began to get the impression that things were cool between Kristan and me. He even put the word out that he didn't want anymore beef with me. On more than one occasion I saw Kristan and his bodyguard, Jamie, in different places. They would wave and say, "What's up Rock Hard? How are you, my brother?"

There was never any tension, therefore, I assumed that all was good between us. I was wrong. Kristan had rocked me to sleep, and just when I thought the ugly shit was behind us, it was only just beginning.

I was up at Bowery High School, hanging out with my lady's brother, Pablo, when shit got funky. We were sitting on the lowest steps of the school when Kristan pulled up in his gray Jetta. As he was getting out of his vehicle, he removed his jewelry, and put on the expression of a guy looking for trouble.

I thought, *I know this skinny dude does not want to fight with me.* I looked around to see who his target might be, but I saw no one else who could pose a threat to him.

I took stock of my situation. Unfortunately, where Pablo and I sat, rows of hedges to the right and left of us blocked our view of his uncle, Surgical, and his crew exiting two other vehicles. Kristan kept his distance from me until his crew was beside him, and that's when I knew there was going to be a problem.

Kristan eventually moved toward me, aggressively. "What's up with that beef, Rock Hard?"

I stood up. "You squashed the beef."

"Nah man, none of that got squashed," He smirked.

All at once, I was attacked from all directions. I fought with every inch of my life while taking a horrific beating. My motto at that time was to never run from anyone after punches were thrown. I stood my ground and fought seven of West side Bowery's crew.

Kristan sparked a f ire under me that day. The shit he pulled made it clear that my neighborhood and his were still at war. Kristan and his crew had become a problem that needed to be solved.

A bunch of little wars sporadically broke out between Bowery and the Metro Boys— and I mean all over the place. It was going down on sight, and neither side was prepared to back down.

My homeboy, TM, had a fight with one of the Bowery

Boys members on Bowery Street and Storm St. It's been said to have been one of the longest street fights in the Bronx history. TM fought this short, scrappy dude named Don Kawand who lived on Bowery, but had Brooklyn ties with some gangsters from Marlboro houses in Coney Island. They fought for a grueling thirteen minutes throwing pipe-hitting blows.

The reason the duration of the fight was estimated at thirteen minutes was that it delayed the BX2 bus. The fight started on Storm St. and Stonewall Ave., but eventually spilled out onto the bus terminal grounds. Because of the growing crowd of onlookers, several buses couldn't move. Overall, TM won that fight, although they both got some good licks in, and both their faces were badly bashed up.

Later that week, Kristan and Blue-Eyed Bully drove through Metropolitan shooting at anyone who was out hustling. They managed to hit Brody Cherry, a Metro Boys member known as a tough gunman in the neighborhood. This kind of behavior went back and forth for a good while.

In the middle of it all, my f irst love, Fabiana Suarez, became pregnant in October of 1987. My situation got a bit tougher with her carrying my child, while Kristan and his Bowery Boys wanted my head. I did my best to just go to work and stay out of trouble, but I couldn't shake the out-of-control beef between Bowery and Metro.

It appeared that it was not going to be over until one of us was being carried by six, while the other was being judged by twelve.

14

I Am Rock Hard

Being on the block continued to become progressively more threatening. Not only did I have to worry about Fabiana, but my three younger sisters, as well. Two of them were already attending High School, and the other was headed there the following year. My mother was always on my case about staying clear of the war between West Side Bowery, the Bronx, and Metropolitan, but I couldn't. I *started* it.

Moms even tried getting me out of the neighborhood by taking me with her and a close friend of the family, Ms. Donna Taylor, to Atlantic City, New Jersey for the weekend.

We were staying at the Taj Mahal Casino Hotel and had a room on the 5th floor with a balcony that displayed a picturesque view of the ocean. It was one of my mother's favorite places. She loved playing the slot machines and gazing upon the ocean views.

It was a beautiful room that we shared for the weekend getaway. That Friday night, and our first evening at the casino, we had a good meal and gambled until about 2 AM before calling it a night. The room had two beds. My mother slept in the one by the balcony, Ms. Donna had the other, and I slept on a cot on the floor.

It was about 9 AM when I awoke to the most beautiful image I had ever laid eyes on in my life. My Earth Angel, my mother, the finest woman I have ever met, was standing near the glass door that led to the balcony just staring out into the ocean.

The glare of the sun was shining on her pretty face and I couldn't help but to stare at her as she seemed to be at peace. Once she noticed that I was awake she softly said, "Hey boy."

"Good morning mom."

"How did you sleep?" She replied still staring out at the ocean with her hands behind her back and barely moving.

"Good," I responded as she slightly nodded her head and continued to gaze aimlessly at the view of the Atlantic Ocean.

"There's not too much time left on this earth Swithun," my mother spoke softly.

"Come again," I responded, not quite sure what she said or what she meant.

"The souls from the past are coming to shore."

"Mom, just what is it that you're trying to say?" I curiously questioned.

"Come here son," she said while motioning with her left hand for me to stand next to her.

I did as she said and once by her side, she placed her

hand on my shoulder and said, "Stay still. And look closely."
As I focused on the view, I began to see silhouettes of souls
slowly walking up on the shore from the Atlantic Ocean. It
frightened me so much that I jerked back from my mother's
touch. "Don't be afraid, Swithun. You have the gift as well."

It was easy for my mother to say but I was truly frightened
at what I was witnessing. I then explained to my mother that
I was aware of my gift and that I had seen ghosts before but
not like what I was experiencing at that moment.

"Wait, when you're not sinning the way you are, sleeping
with more than one woman, drinking and hanging with the
crowd you be around your gift will become clearer." My
mother explained, but it was something that I didn't want.

I enjoyed that weekend with my mother and the
experience we shared together was something I'd never
mentioned to anyone. She only wanted what was best for
me, so I did my best to focus on just going to work at the
Race Track once we returned back to Bronx.

Working kept me off the block, and my mother was
more than excited after seeing me on television. I got lucky,
and was proud to work the 1987 Preakness Race, at Pimlico,
in Maryland.

J. Clinton Hawthorne had a two-year-old black stallion
horse named "Stall Them" in that race. Mr. Sammy, the
Assistant Trainer, asked me to join the team for the trip. He
told me I'd be away for a couple of days, and that I would
be getting a ride to and from Maryland. I'd be riding in J.
Clinton's horse van along with Jerry, Stall Them's groomer,
and another caretaker whose name I can't recall.

We had a good time riding down to Maryland, playing
cards and discussing our relationships with women. I
brought along a bag of goodies: some cold cuts, American
cheese and sandwich spread, as well as some of my favorite

junk foods. My goodie bag was not complete without a cold soda. I was more than excited to be on the road, and far from the neighborhood beef.

I shared my food with the other two guys and in return Jerry treated me to Friday's restaurant once we made it to our destination and got settled in. Afterward, I slept in front of Stall Them's stall to ensure that the horse was good. The following morning, I found the men's shower room, where I got myself a hot shower and slipped into something comfortable.

Jerry and I both brought decent suits to wear along with some very nice shoes. We had our gear laid out in a nearby shed room, ready to be worn. At least that's what our plan was.

J. Clinton Hawthorne's wife walked past our room and saw our clothing lying on a stack of hay and *she* immediately changed our plans. Mrs. Hawthorne disappeared for a few moments and then returned with two ugly, yellow golf T-shirts with a horse's image and the words *"Annual Preakness Race"* on the front left. She also brought matching baseball caps for us to wear to ensure that we didn't outshine her husband. So, Jerry and I wore our new yellow attire with our dirty work jeans.

The rich were just different. That was for sure.

To make matters worse, Stall Them lost the Preakness, but not before my mother spotted me on national TV. As soon as she did, she went through the roof yelping, "Rock Hard! There goes Rock Hard! He's on TV!"

My siblings ran into the living room where our mother continued screaming with Annabell pride.

When I thought the beef between Westside Bowery and the Metropolitan was finally settling down again—it started brewing once more. This time, the girls from Bowery decided to get in on it, too. While I was trying to make changes for the better in my life, things only got worse.

My three younger sisters, Gabriella, Violet, and Penelope, were on their way home from Spellman High in Ridgewood, Bronx, when they met trouble head-on. They were riding the BX56 bus, and when they made it to Bowery, Bronx, decided to go shopping for shoes. It was something they wanted to do before making their way to the BX2 bus that would take them to Metropolitan Avenue.

Some of Kristan's crew, along with their rough-neck girlfriends, were hanging out on Storm St., at the Plaza Mall. As my sisters approached the Plaza, one of the girls pointed at my sisters, and said, "Ain't they from Metropolitan?"

The entire group followed my sisters into the Plaza. My friend, Alfonso Sancho, who worked in a sneaker booth inside the Plaza, saw the commotion and ordered the crowd to back up off my sisters.

That didn't work out too well. One of the girls shoved Violet, and Violet punched her in the face. Alfonso managed to keep my youngest sister, Gabriella, safe while Violet and Penelope went back out of the Plaza to fight.

God blessed me with a strong sixth sense, because I felt the trouble ahead of time. I was making my way up to the Storm St. Mall at the exact time my sisters needed me the most. While making my way through the bus terminal, I ran into a good friend, my homeboy, Haitian Ace. Ace was a good-looking brother with light-skin and hazel eyes, a real chick magnet. He also had a damn good knuckle game.

As soon as Haitian Ace and I approached the Storm St. Mall, we ran into a large crowd of spectators watching my sisters battle it out with the Bowery girls. Ace and I ran towards the crowd where I finally caught a glimpse of

Penelope in the thick of it. My heart turned cold at the sight of my sisters scrapping.

Once she saw me and Ace, she shouted, "Now, bitches!" and started pounding on one of the Bowery girls. Penelope was under the false impression that Ace and I had a large crew with us when she saw the crowd behind us running toward the fight to see what was going down. Unfortunately, it was only the two of us.

Ace and I wasted no time jumping in, and boy did we have our hands full. We fought long and hard with guys and girls alike. They attacked us from all sides. Violet had a heavyset, light-skinned girl's hair wrapped around her fist, and that girl clutched and yanked at my sister's shirt.

I heard Violet screaming, "I can't see! They maced me!" I pulled the girl off of Violet, and told her to hold on to the back of my shirt. Now, Ace and I held them back with both of my sisters safely behind us.

The crowd closed in for their second wave of attack. When a dark- skinned, fella pulled a gun, I knew I had to step it up.

I screamed, with authority, "I am Rock Hard from Metropolitan Avenue! If you continue any further, there will be repercussions!"

Ace and I prepared for another round, but instead we heard a series of fearful whispers as they finally began to back off.

"That's Rock Hard from Metropolitan." A soft, female voice said.

"Yo chill… That's Rock Hard…," several male voices echoed in the crowd.

One by one, they walked away. Within seconds, we had a clear path to the bus terminal. I could not believe my eyes, nor did I realize that my reputation was that heavy.

In any case, they had drawn first blood on my family, and that meant *WAR*.

Once I got back to the neighborhood, I assembled a meeting with the majority of the Metro Boys. We wanted blood. It was bad enough that Kristan had managed to shoot a few members of our Metro Boys, but jumping my sisters was like throwing gasoline on an already-blazing f lame.

After the meeting, while walking down Metropolitan Avenue from Heart St. toward Voice St., I bumped into DJ Sky Bay. Bay was a well-respected Elder in our neighborhood. He was pretty tight with my oldest sister, Isabella, and my brother, Freddie. So, he kind of had that big brother thing for me. Bay wasn't too fond of what was going on in the 'hood because of me.

The last time he had bumped into me, I had been cutting classes with another kid from IS 219 Junior High, and had just finished joyriding in the Principal's car. He knew I could be going down the wrong path, so he had started lecturing me about the whole Bowery-Metro Boys beef back then.

This time, he said, "Rock Hard, this is nothing new. The beef between Bowery and Metro has been going on since way back before your time, but never have I seen it on the level it's reached since you got involved. Don't let this stupid shit go to your head, you need to make a U-turn from it all when given a chance."

"But Bay, I have a job at Speedway Race Track. I don't even hustle for Wolfman anymore. I've been staying away from the streets, but this situation keeps haunting me somehow." I complained, frustrated that I couldn't get away from the foolishness.

"I heard through the grapevine that the war was on hot and heavy because of you." He placed both of his hands on my shoulders, and in a strong, solemn voice went on, "Rock

Hard I don't want anything to happen to you. I witness a lot of death on these streets. It ain't worth it! Believe me, brother!"

His last comment struck a nerve, and for a moment it had me thinking on how we were going to get this beef behind us. The only solution I could come up with was war. There was no other way. We had to defeat West Side Bowery, Bronx once and for all.

After DJ Sky Bay had leaned into me about how much death he witnessed in the streets of the Bronx, I couldn't help but remember the death of my friend, young Cipriano Junior, the son of the salsa King Cipriano Deleon Senior. I started having flashbacks about his death.

Cipriano Junior had been born October 19, 1968 to Cipriano Deleon and Yesenia Deleon. On June 23, 1983, Cipriano Junior had been shot to death on Spark St. and Metropolitan Avenue. One of our homeboys, Mateo, had been mishandling a firearm, and accidentally shot him.

Mateo had removed the magazine from his .380 semi-automatic pistol and pulled back the slide with his finger on the trigger. The ejection rod had not pulled the round out of the chamber. Mateo let the slide go while holding the trigger back, and the round accidentally discharged and hit Cipriano in the side.

It had happened in Justin's basement apartment. Cipriano had run upstairs, dropped on the living room floor, and started turning blue. He died en route to the hospital.

When you're a teenager and death hits close to home like that, everyone feels the pain, whether they're close to that person or not.

Anxiety had played a big part in my teenage years as

far as protecting my family and Fabiana went. I remember saying to myself, *"Why couldn't I have a regular life? And a father around to teach me better and keep me and my siblings safe?"*

By the time I got back home, my mother had the answer for me. As I reached the front door, my mother yelled down the stairs to me, "Grab that Ginger Ale out of the refrigerator and bring it upstairs with you!"

I did as she said and made my way up to her bedroom. She didn't look up at me, but had her eyes set in the Holy Bible, as usual. Before I could say anything, she told me "You did not choose, you were chosen. That battle against Satan, which is the principal task of St. Michael, God's Arch Angel, is still being fought on a daily basis because Satan is still alive and active in the world." She finally raised her eyes to meet mine adding, "Out of all my children, you are smack dead in the middle of that battle. There was war in the kingdom of God. There will always be war, until the end of time."

From that statement, and things heating up between Metropolitan Avenue and Bowery, I knew it was going to be a tough battle.

She said, "You have a big heart, Swithun Junior, but you can't save the world. Keep your prayers up, especially before you fight. You will have protection that nobody can see, not even you!"

15

Presence of Death

The next day, everything mother had said weighed heavily on my mind. When I left work that afternoon, her words followed me home.

I had just got back to the neighborhood, and was crossing Metropolitan Avenue and Voice St., when I heard the payphone on the corner ringing.

Something made me answer the ringing payphone, and when I did I got the surprise of a lifetime. It was Ethan Lite calling from Dannemora, New York's Clinton correctional facility, a New York state penitentiary. In the mid-80's in the inner-city, brothers on lock-down were able to call payphones in their neighborhoods. With any luck, someone they knew would answer.

What were the odds of me, of all people, answering that

call from Michael Lite? It had to be one in a million, or a blessing from God that I didn't recognize at the moment. I was happy as all heck to hear the familiar voice of my brother from another mother.

"What's up, Big Ethan?" I proclaimed. "How's a heavyweight like yourself holding up?"

"I'm living pretty good nowadays thanks to Mad Rapper!"

Apparently, Ethan was looking out for most of the roughnecks from Bronx, in the penitentiary. Just as he had run the show on Rikers Island, he was running things in Clinton. Ethan lucked up when Black Bear, a close friend of Mad Rapper, the famous Rapper from Graham Boulevard, in Bronx, happened to come through Ethan's house.

On the strength of Ethan knowing both him and Mad Rapper, he had Ethan's protection. In return, Mad Rapper started supporting him. Mad Rapper also promised Big Ethan a job as his bodyguard when he got out of jail.

"Ethan, how much more time do you have?" I curiously questioned.

"I got about a year and three months."

"That's not so bad." Was all I could think about saying at the moment.

"Rock Hard, this is not a place for any of us. We were just trying to survive. The system is a setup for us inner-city kids. But all in all, this is not a place for the weak. Only the strong survive here. Other than that, I've been hearing a lot about you on the streets. What's good with you?"

"Ethan I have a family to protect," I replied, surprised that he was on top of what was going on in Metropolitan.

"Ain't that the truth. How many are you right now?"

"I think it's about 11 of us."

Ethan started laughing hard, and jokingly said, "That means it's about 12 of y'all!"

We both laughed.

"Your mother really loves kids," Ethan said.

"Yes, she does."

"I know you have to go, but be careful, my brother! I received a letter from my man last week, about that beef you got going on. It's poppin' off on Rikers Island, too."

"Wow, that's crazy! But believe it or not, I have a job at Speedway Race Track, and Fabiana and I are expecting a child."

"No way, dude!" Ethan responded.

"Yes way my brother! Times are changing for the better. I'm trying to do right, but the devil keeps trying me."

"Keep away from those streets. I'll be home soon."

"Okay, continue being strong my brother. I'll see you soon enough."

I had a huge Kool-Aid smile on my face when I hung up the phone, and if someone was looking, they probably thought I was crazy. I was talking to myself out loud from the excitement of hearing my boy's voice. But knowing that the beef I was having was also taking place on Rikers Island concerned me. Things were getting out of control and I had a baby on the way to start thinking about.

When I got home, my mother started lecturing me as if she was on the line during my conversation with Ethan. "He was not lying about prison. It's not a place for no one."

My eyes widened at her statement. *How did she know?*

She continued, "You are about to have a big fight very soon, and what did I tell you to do before going into battle?"

"Pray, lots of prayer, Mommy."

"That's right, my son, right before a battle, right?" She questioned, looking for confirmation.

"Right, Mother." I quickly acknowledged.

"Guess what, Swithun Junior? You are always in a battle for you are the *Chosen One*. So, you must always pray, my son."

And right she was because I would get lost in the world from time to time, but only because we're born into a life of sin. That evening, I repented my sins and went heavily into prayer asking my *Father Who Art in Heaven* to accept me as a child of His, and to protect me as I walk through the valley of the shadow of death, and to strengthen my heart so I would fear no evil.

Father of the Kingdom, be the Lord of my strength, which teacheth my hands to war and my fingers to fight. Father Almighty, I am not a perfect young man. I have many weaknesses. Please, my Lord, give me time to grow wise in Jesus name. Amen!

I tried to continue on with my daily routine, with work and all, but my sixth sense kept warning me that a huge battle was imminent. *I knew it.* I *felt* the presence of death creeping around corners, waiting to pounce. It was a feeling that I dreaded, although it gave me the advantage of choice. I could lay low and not engage in conflict, or at least know when to prepare for the unavoidable battles.

Around that time I took a ride to New Town, which was a part of Bowery, and there too I picked up the stench of impending death. That evening, I went to check on my boys, Alfonso Sancho and Floyd. Upon arrival, I saw a bunch of rough looking dudes at the corner of their block. Alfonso and Floyd, along with our homie, Daryl, were in the middle of the block with their crew, as well. When I got out of the car Alfonso warned me about the dudes at the corner. Floyd was pulling on leather gloves, which meant a one-on-one fight was about to take place. As it turned out, Floyd had a beef with some punks from the neighborhood, and he was about to put hands on some wannabe named Jason. He was with his crew, Champagne, Prince, Gary, and a few other fellas that I didn't know, when they came toward us.

My boy, Floyd, snuffed Jason off his feet before he could even get into his fighting stance. Alfonso, Daryl and I, along with Jason's crew, watched them go one-on-one for a little bit. The whole time I was haunted by that eerie sensation of death's breath washing over us. I wondered, *Could this be it? Could this situation right here and now be it? Because, if so, I need it to be over and done with.*

While Floyd was scrapping with Jason, I smacked the tastebuds out of Fat Gary because he was just standing too close to me. I slapped him so hard that his knees buckled. By the time he composed himself and decided to step towards me, Daryl stepped in and dropped him with a five-punch combination. Gary hit the concrete like a sack of rocks. His eyes rolled back in his head, and he began convulsing.

My boy, Alfonso, quickly engaged in a bout with Jason's boy, Prince. Before we knew it, there was a full-fledged rumble in the middle of Smoke St. in New Town. Jason, Champagne, and Prince were the most aggressive out of their crew, but were no match for us. We had them on the run from Alfonso and Floyd's block to Bellhop Avenue and Westside Bowery Bronx as we poured onto the middle of Bellhop Avenue.

Jason and his crew tried to take one more stand against us, but the lions in our blood stepped up for the *Coup De Grâce*. Victory was near. We were not going to accept defeat because there was no pact between lions and men. We intended to finish them off with any and everything we could get our hands on.

Floyd flipped over a garbage can and started tossing bottles. Alfonso picked up the other garbage can and rushed at them while Daryl and I threw bottles and rocks before finally backing them down with some sticks we'd found in the trash.

We were amped up when New York's Finest arrived on the scene, and the adrenaline burning through our veins had us ready to get it on with *them*, too. At least six patrol cars with flashing lights pulled up, and when their doors opened, at least a dozen cops jumped out ready for action. Most of them had their blue steel .38 caliber Specials drawn, while the others were armed with nightsticks.

No one wanted to back down, but Floyd yelled, "Don't give them the pleasure!"

We had to pull each other away from the mangle before we ended up suffering the wrath of the NYPD. It only took a second for reality to kick in and for us to engage in what we called *Back Yard Olympics*. We took off running between houses, jumping over a few backyard fences, and across a few garages, in order to get away from the cops that were now chasing us.

Once back on Alfonso and Floyd's block, we celebrated with forty ounces of Olde English beer. I proposed a toast to our victory over the chumps we had defeated. We made sure to pour some beer onto the ground for our fallen inner-city warriors before drinking. It was good to respect our dead, something we got from the 70's movie *Cooley High*.

I eventually departed from my brothers after a wild and crazy night. I couldn't help but notice that the presence of death was still riding me, and it started to get even heavier.

Once at home, I started preparing for work the next day.

I left the bathroom after showering, and was on my way to the door that led to my man cave in the basement when my mother bellowed from the second floor, "Swithun!"

"Yes, Mom."

"Come here!"

I spun around and headed upstairs to her bedroom. As expected, there my mother sat, on her bed, with the Bible on her lap. She glanced up at me, smiled, and then started to preach.

"Whenever you are in a war, you are in the presence of death. Even in the physical form, a boxer or karate fighter is in the presence of death when fighting. You, my son, do both spiritual and physical battles—and yes, is the answer. War is upon you and most of the neighborhood."

I stood there, listening carefully to every word that rolled off her tongue.

She ended her sermon with, "Now, good night, Swithun. I know you have to work in the morning."

I crossed the narrow space to give her a good night kiss. "Good night, Mother."

The following morning I jumped up and got dressed for work. Craig Hopper, a.k.a. Redd, who was a buddy of mine, met me on Bane St. and Metropolitan Avenue. He wanted a job at Speedway Race Track, so we walked together to J. Clinton Hawthorne racing stable.

Along the way, we talked about Ethan Lite and all that was going on in and out of the neighborhood. To tell you the truth, crack spots all sounded the same—shoot-outs every other night, dead bodies here, and dead bodies there.

I said, "When does it end?"

He responded with the only answer he could. "Everything has its ending, but it seems like, when the government wants it done. If you think about it, they're doing a good job of keeping our people down."

"If they wanted to stop it they could. Their so-called military can travel overseas to a foreign country for the sole purpose of oil and other resources. I mean, they take over city by city within a couple of weeks, but they can't stop a drug problem in the inner cities?" I said.

"It's because they don't want to. It keeps the dark faces incarcerated, and keeps the system going with arrests" Craig said, as we made our way to the race track, both feeling disappointed at how the system had inner-city families caught in the struggle.

"Damn if you don't have a point, my brother." I agreed, as we continued toward our destination: Work.

We had both witnessed a great deal of injustice, not only in our neighborhood, but throughout the entire city, on a regular basis.

Finally, after reaching the main entrance to the backstretch of Speedway Race Track, Mr. Sammy agreed to give Craig a shot at working with us.

After a call was made to Barn #52, Craig was issued a temporary ID from security. After three days, he was sent to the main office, where he was fingerprinted and processed, which meant he got the job. As it turned out, Mr. Sammy liked the way Craig worked. He even gave him a nickname, Al Green—after the legendary R&B singer from the 70's. Every time my coworkers and I heard Mr. Sammy refer to him as Al Green, we would crack up laughing.

After about two weeks on the job, Craig had grown familiar with the Mexicans, and would clown around with them throughout the day. Craig knew that I spoke a little

Spanish, and one day he pulled me to the side and asked, "How do you say fuck you in Spanish?"

"Da me la pinga." I smiled.

Redd began yelling at every Mexican in Barn #52. It wasn't until Mr. Sammy heard him saying it that he found out what it really meant. Mr. Sammy asked, "Al Green, what are you saying to these guys?"

"Fuck you, in Spanish," Craig confidently responded.

"No. You're telling them to give you their dicks."

Craig was angry as hell, and just as embarrassed. He was as "Redd" as his nickname.

As soon as we finished making our rounds, Redd grabbed a white plastic stick that had a little weight to it, and started chasing me all around the outside of the barn. I was running and laughing while he cursed me out. Once he caught up with me, my back was on fire from him whacking me with the plastic stick. It hurt like hell, but I could not stop laughing. He had been so damn easy to pull one over on. It was like shooting f lies with a canon.

At home, I had a surprise waiting for me. My baby girl, Fabiana, was there and looking good as usual. As I came in the door, she threw her arms around me and gave me a sensational kiss— I mean, eyes closed, tongues wrestling, and the exchange of genuine emotions between two people in love.

"Rock Hard, you stink! Go and take a bath. You smell like a horse." Fabiana laughed.

"I was at work, and not horsing around."

We laughed for a moment which took away that troubling sensation of death's breath that seemed to roll over me all the time lately. Then, in an instant, it threatened me again.

After I cleaned up, Fabiana and I went to the Chinese

restaurant to get something to eat. We rented a movie before returning to my man cave. Halfway through the movie, I got a little frisky. One thing led to another, and we ended up breaking a sweat until we were both satisfied.

While lying in my arms, my girl began to explain that she was having a tough time at home with her parents. Apparently, they were not too fond of her being pregnant and not married at seventeen. I kissed her on her forehead, pulled her close, and whispered, "Everything is going to be okay."

I did my best to assure her that I was going to take care of her and my baby. I believe she felt a little better after I mentioned getting a higher paying job and a place for us to live. She stopped crying for a moment, and after wiping tears from her eyes she said something that brought back the ugly feeling I'd been having for weeks.

"I almost forgot to tell you that the word is out that if the Bowery girls or boys catch anyone from Metropolitan on Bowery Street, they're going to get jumped."

"Where are you getting this shit from?" I growled.

"From my friend, Kim. You remember her? You beat her brother up at Bowery high school."

"How long ago did she tell you this?"

"About two weeks ago."

I rose up off the bed and looked her dead in her eyes. "Baby, why are you telling me this so late? Do you have any idea how serious this is, Fabiana?"

"Do you know how serious our pregnancy is?" She swiftly shot back.

"You got a point, Mama, but I have to protect you as well, baby." I immediately changed the subject. I told Fabiana what I had done to Redd at work, and her tears turned into laughter. She couldn't believe I had done such a thing to him of all people. Redd had some local fame back then. He used to battle break dancers and moonwalkers. In fact, he beat a well-known Bee Boy that had a part in the motion picture, "Beat Street." I mean, the brother held his own, when it came to performing.

Redd and another Bee Boy, Pablo, were asked to dance for our neighborhood's own Two Mic's, but as Redd put it to me—*"the money wasn't right."* He made more money on the streets dancing than they could ever offer him. Redd and I were pretty tight although we mostly only hung out together at work. He also was aware of my spirituality, and never judged me on it.

Later that evening, I took Fabiana home in a cab. In fact, whenever she came over, it was the same routine. I brought her home in a taxi, and took the same cab back to my place.

The following day after work, while Redd and I were walking home, I mentioned that after Fabiana and I became pregnant I stopped talking to my sidekick, Nora, and had also been out of touch with Guadalupe.

Redd stopped walking, and started singing, "Here comes the bride, all dressed in white..."

All I could do was laugh. It was always good talking to my friend before and after work.

As soon as I made it home and walked through the front door, my mother called me upstairs. Before I could get past the threshold, Mom shouted, "Do not touch your baby brother before washing the horses off of you!"

I started laughing really hard, and she said, "What's so funny?"

I explained to her what Redd and I discussed earlier and everything from there on became very comical. After taking a shower, I went back to my mother's room and picked up my baby brother, Ethan. My mother, without glancing toward me, said, "You're about to go to war. Prepare yourself."

Mom was always right, so I started to inform many of our crew from Metropolitan Avenue as well as some of the Belvedere Boulevard crew.

That evening I received a call from Fabiana. She sounded frightened as she rambled on incoherently about something or other.

"Ruby," I called her by her nickname, "calm down, sweetie, and tell me what's been said."

Kim had told Fabiana that all of the Bowery Boys would be up on Bowery Street tomorrow, and that they would be looking to jump anyone from Metropolitan—guys and girls alike. Also, Kristan and some of his crew had gone to Metropolitan Avenue the night before with intentions of doing some drive-by shootings, but got stopped by the 48th Precinct instead. The Officers had conducted a search and found two 12-gauge, pump-action shotguns as well as three 9mm pistols.

Apparently, they had been placed under arrest and jailed in the Bronx house of detention. After facing the judge, Kristan was sent to Rikers Island to await trial.

Supposedly, upon arrival at Rikers, Kristan placed a call back to his people in West Bowery, Bronx. He was trying to make bail preparations, and ordered them to commit gang assaults on anyone from Metropolitan Avenue whether they were affiliated with a crew or not.

The whole thing sounded pretty far-fetched to me. I mean, Kristan, a skinny punk drug dealer from Bowery, ordering a whole entire neighborhood to act on his behalf all in a retaliatory effort to deepen the beef between him and me? *Yeah, right!* I thought. But, as a precaution, I assembled a big enough crew to go up to Bowery Street the following day.

I didn't want to take a chance on my lady or unborn child being attacked, nor our family or other friends. Kristan had upped the ante and bloodshed was inevitable. That night I got down on my knees, locked my hands together, and with my eyes closed, I prayed that the bloodshed would not lead to death.

16

Bloody War

The next morning, Redd called to let me know that he was going to be absent from J. Clinton Hawthorne's racing stable. His old man, Craig Hopper Sr., owned and operated a construction company that mostly specialized in demolition, and had asked him to give him a hand on his job. So, I had to take the hike to Speedway Race Track on my own, and boy did it feel lonely. That bad vibe rode my back the whole way there.

After putting in a hard day's work, I went home, cleaned up, and made some phone calls. I had to make sure there were enough of us heading to the Storm St. Plaza Mall on Bowery Street. My boy, "Little L," couldn't make the trip with me and the crew, so he brought over a 12-gauge pump shotgun with a pistol grip, and a chrome .32 caliber Python revolver, just in case things got funky around the way again.

Some of our crew were already waiting on Metropolitan Avenue with about twenty close friends and allies lined up in front of my house. While waiting for me to exit, they showed my family a great deal of respect. When I stepped onto my porch, a feeling of honor and love overwhelmed me at the sight of those ready for battle.

Walking out my front door felt as if I had stepped out of the White House accompanied by the US Military. Everyone greeted me as I slowly descended the stairs of my porch onto the pavement. Paola, a tough homegirl with pretty caramel skin and long beautiful hair was on the curb. She had a crew of girls who were ready to rumble.

Paola gave me a big hug. "I would not dream of missing this. Me and my girls are with you in this battle."

Our elders stood outside watching while others watched us from their windows. We marched up Metropolitan Avenue with fire in our eyes. Once we made it to the corner of Voice St., more of my homeboys merged into the mix. Majestic, Larry, and Pee Funk were extra soldiers, and the sight of them, standing tall and ready for battle, brought me a little comfort.

Larry said, "Where do you think you're going without us?"

"Nowhere without you, Larry," I responded, and then all three of them gave me a strong hug.

Pee Funk hollered, "Metro Boys!"

Immediately after he said that we all yelled out, "We're the Metro Boys! Not a gang, but a bloodline!"

The moment was so real, it nearly brought tears to my eyes. The love everyone was showing me over a beef that started years ago between Kristan and me had touched my soul. Things had gotten a little out of control, but in my mind it was going to be settled today once and for all.

We started our journey by marching up Metropolitan Avenue towards Bane St. with some of our most notorious crew members patiently awaiting our arrival. As we were approaching Bane St. I spotted my boy Big Roe. I could see the excitement in his body language when he noticed me approaching with at least thirty-strong behind me. He tossed both fists up in the air as if he'd just won a fifteen-round championship bout. He was bouncing and skipping around like Mohammed Ali, eager to get it on with the Bowery Boys.

As we stepped onto the sidewalk of Bane and Metropolitan Ave., Till Morning, a.k.a. TM, came out of Sal's pizzeria walking with the swagger you can only pick up from our hood. Behind him was Pimp, another rough-neck from Metropolitan, my dude Party Boy, who lived for a good fistfight, and Crow, Coffee, and a few other crew members.

We had a brief discussion about sticking together the best way we could if we were to go into battle. That presence of death feeling was pressing down hard on me now. I knew we were going into war the minute we got onto Storm St., but I didn't share it with anyone. Being spiritual enough to sense a tragedy wasn't something I could readily speak about. It was just something I silently carried.

About thirty-seven of us waited to board the BX2 bus that would take us to Storm St. Since there were so many of us, we knew we'd have trouble boarding any bus, so three of us stood visible at the bus stop, while the rest of us hid around the corner.

Within minutes, a bus pulled up and stopped. The front door opened, and two of our guys went to the front as if they were going to pay, but really were just going to keep the bus driver from closing the doors on us. The third crew member went to the back door. After a middle-aged lady exited the back of the bus, he held the back door open.

With both bus doors open, the rest of us immediately came out of hiding and rushed onto the bus using both entrances. We poured into the bus like the wild bunch of teenagers that we were. There was very little respect for the driver or any remaining passengers.

Back then there were no signs on the front of the buses that lit up saying *"Call the Police,"* so the driver was stuck with us for the ride. There was a sense of calmness among us, until we got to our stop.

It was a little after three in the afternoon, and the sun was breaking through some clouds when we made it to the bus terminal on Throne Boulevard. Before going any further, we made sure everyone was together as we prepared to cut to Storm St. Mall.

I was front and center as we boldly marched toward Storm St. to invade the Bowery Boys' comfort, and cause pain to as many as possible. I was caught in the moment and didn't even notice that my oldest brother, Freddie, was with us. He appeared out of nowhere to my left. We made eye contact but neither of us said a word. He was still wearing his apron from Waldbaum's Supermarket. Freddie worked in the meat department and had actually traveled from Jerusalem Turnpike in Brooklyn County with blood stains on his apron.

Before I could ask him how he knew about what was going on, I felt a tap on my right shoulder. I turned to find Miles, one of my older cousins from Brooklyn, smiling at me. He was one musclebound dude who didn't mind a good brawl.

Under the circumstances having family by my side was an added bonus. As we continued our journey to Storm St. I was processing everything that might come at me and everything around me. Then, I thought, *I wonder who orchestrated my family's arrival.* Maybe it was from my mother's mouth to God's ear.

Once we finally reached Storm St., I couldn't believe my eyes. It was a surreal moment of *Yea, though I walk through the valley of the shadow of death, I will fear no evil.* Shit. We were outnumbered by at least three-to-one. I had truly underestimated that skinny punk, Kristan! West side Bowery crew were on both sides of Storm St., Mall, at least one hundred and fifty strong.

A few more of our crew met us halfway as we poured into the middle of the street at Storm St. Mall. Someone had a boom box and it was going full blast. The loud sound of the lyrics to *Rock Box* by Two Mic's was playing as if it was our pre-battle theme song. It couldn't have been more fitting to be listening to a group that came from Metropolitan Avenue before we clashed.

The Bowery Boys started shouting and taunting us. The store merchants began to quickly pull down the metal gates to their stores in order to protect their merchandise before all hell broke loose. It was clear to everyone that the Metro Boys meant business.

I don't recall who threw the first punch. The Metro Boys and Bowery Boys clashed into a battle like ancient Gladiators out of a history book. There was a big dude with braids advancing upon me. When he got within arm's reach, I swung a hard right to the side of his face. I thought I had caught him with a pretty good shot, but the dude's fighting skills were up to par. I tried to put him out with one blow, but he immediately retaliated with a three-punch combination that sent me reeling.

Running was not an option, so I quickly composed myself. Not only did I see his three-punch combo, but I added an extra two for good measure. The five-punch combination that I returned had knocked him on his ass. This was not a fictional movie with special effects, so when he went down, he went down hard.

That was just a small reminder that I was from Metropolitan, and I hadn't come to play *Ring Around The Rosie*. Everyone that lived on the Bowery side was our enemy the night prior, and our enemies still. Dude was on the ground when the beast inside of me took control of my body.

With no mercy in my heart, and teeth bared like a lion, I began to kick and stomp dude's face into the pavement. Blood was oozing out of a cut on his forehead, but before I could finish him off, one of his comrades came to his rescue.

Someone delivered a mighty blow to my mouth and jaw. It was so severe that I felt as if I was out cold while standing on my feet. But, in that moment, I was still conscious of the battle taking place around me. It was as if time stood still. I could see the spirits in everyone fighting as well as the souls of the past that kept coming and going throughout the battlefield. All this while a hundred and eighty modern-day warriors broke the boundaries of a peace that would never be…not around here anyway.

Innocent passers-by were trying to get out of the way, but were being trampled. Even kids from both crews were being stepped on and stepped over during the melee. I caught a quick glimpse of TM punching two of the Bowery Boys in the face. Big Roe was only a few feet away from me when he scooped up this one dude and body-slammed him into a wall.

Everything was happening fast, and although I was in the midst of battle, I had the presence of mind to notice the NYPD strobe lights f lashing in my peripheral vision. The lights were flashing, but no sirens were sounding off. It appeared that they were just watching because they were on the scene, but did nothing to stop us.

I had no idea where my last opponent disappeared to and that was lucky for him because I was still in beast mode. Meanwhile, my homegirl, Paola, and her crew were getting it on with some grown men because the girls from West Bowery were no match for them. When I noticed Paola tussling with this one dude, I hurried over to help her out. I caught him off guard and punched him in the head, almost breaking my hand. He stumbled, but was able to give me a run for my money. We were going at it blow for blow.

Paola got overcome by two roughneck dudes from the Bowery side. They knocked her to the ground, grabbed her by the arms and legs, then swung her into a wall, and I couldn't do a damn thing about it. I was facing an opponent much bigger than I, and had to give him every bit of my attention. I was engaged in a serious bout as was everyone around me.

This battle seemed to go on forever. The NYPD simultaneously formed a large task force that had the neighboring precincts backing up the 48th Precinct. The 40th precinct from the Cross Bronx came in as well as the 44th Precinct from the Bronx Village. They had mounted up with helmets, nightsticks, and shields. They posted up on the corners of Stonewall Ave. and Storm St. as well as Bowery Street and Storm St.

Everyone was still fighting. I managed to get the

attention of a few of my crew members to inform them that the NYPD was about to try and f lank us. When the NYPD made their move, they came in from Bowery Street quickly and ruthlessly. We were forced towards Stonewall Ave. by police officers in riot gear. They also had about three German shepherds in front of them.

They were steering us right toward a bunch of other police officers in riot gear and paddy wagons that were set up on Stonewall Ave. That was a bad move for them because once the Metro Boys and Bowery Boys realized what was taking place, and that we had no other way out, we all decided to go through the Plaza Mall.

It was chaotic as we rushed toward the glass doors to escape the police. Unfortunately for us, the doors were locked. We grabbed several steel trash cans with the diamond-shaped holes in them, and broke the glass windows and doors.

The NYPD was able to grab a few stragglers, but the looting began before they even knew the windows and glass doors had been broken. Both Metropolitan and Bowery side crews rushed the security guard in the jewelry department. They knocked him out and stole his sidearm before snatching what they could, but I was only focused on getting out of the Mall safely.

In the midst of this commotion, several separate battles had erupted. There were some from each crew who hadn't seen the NYPD through the thick of the crowd until they were under arrest. Others were taken to the hospital by ambulance to be treated for stab wounds, being hit with blunt objects, and so on. The scene was a bloody mess.

A good number of my crew and I escaped via the Plaza Mall by exiting the other side while the police were preoccupied with crowd control. NYPD not only arrested people at the Storm St. Mall, but also went on a search throughout Bronx arresting people for their role in the mayhem. The 48th, 40th, and 44th Precincts were on patrol, stopping any little groups of teenagers that looked as if they were up to no good.

The bunch I got away with did what we knew best— Backyard Olympics. We swiftly traveled through the back streets in between America Avenue and Bowery Street until we reached Anarchy St. and Bowery Street. From there, we trooped it up a hill leading to the Long Island railroad tracks. Once on the track's right-of-way, we were able to run to our block, and then to our homes.

I didn't feel safe until I was back on my block, sweating profusely, and finally feeling the pain in my hands and face from the brawl. I approached my house happy to have made it home, but never expecting to walk in on what I saw. I opened the front door and heard my two oldest sisters' voices loudly and clearly reciting *Psalm 23*.

Their voices grew louder as I curiously made my way up the stairs. Once at the top, I found it kind of odd that my mother's room door was closed. I slowly pushed the door open to f ind my sisters, Isabella and Mia, praying out loud—a frightening scene, similar to something straight out of a horror movie.

Both of them had Bibles in their hands praying over our mother. They both had eyes full of tears and our mother was lying in a scary position not looking like herself. Mia paused long enough to show me a pad that Mom had mustered up enough strength to scribble on earlier, but they couldn't decipher what it said. Mom couldn't speak, and that made matters worse.

I took a close look at what she wrote before becoming

disabled. *"O" "fath"* and *"mc"* was all that was scribbled on the paper. After examining the brief message, I eventually figured it out. She was trying to tell them to go get Father McCoy. He was our priest at St. Pascal Baylon Church, which was right up the block from us on Voice St.

Without wasting another second, I ran down the block to St. Pascal and found Father McCoy in his office. Out of breath, I quickly explained to him the best way that I could that something demonic was going on with my mother. He briefly asked me about her behavior as he put on his priest uniform, then grabbed a Crucifix and some Holy Water before we headed back to my house.

Father McCoy and I rushed up the street while the neighbors looked on in bewilderment, probably because earlier they had seen me marching down Voice St. towards Metropolitan Avenue with an army. Father McCoy began sprinkling Holy Water around the walkway as we approached the front of the house, and continued all the way to the front door.

Once we got through the front door, we could hear my mother loudly screaming, "Nooo!" She was screaming at the top of her lungs, but it wasn't her voice. Father McCoy hit the steps, and I was fast behind him. When he reached the top step he immediately knew what room to go to. He rushed into my mother's room and ordered my sisters to leave immediately. My mother, or should I say whatever was inside of her, constantly screeched, "No, no, no!"

Father McCoy's presence in the room made my mother's body tremble violently as she lay in her bed. It was to the point that the movement started to shake the room. Father McCoy began throwing Holy Water around the room while we watched from the hallway in horror. My mother sat up on the bed, but in the same position she had been lying.

Father McCoy ordered me and my sisters to go downstairs and slammed the door shut. We went down, but could still clearly hear Father McCoy's words: "The Lord is my Light and Salvation. Whom shall I fear? The Lord is the Strength of my life. Of whom shall I be afraid?"

We were frightened out of our minds while we awaited the outcome and prayed for our mother's well-being. We didn't hear her yelling anymore, nor did we feel any further vibration from the room. All we could do was wait patiently and pray.

About three hours had passed, and the sun had gone down by the time Father McCoy came out of the room. My sisters and I ran upstairs, desperately inquiring about what went on with our mother. Father McCoy said it was okay to go into the room and see her. He asked Isabella, my oldest sister, to follow him downstairs so that he could explain what was going on.

Mia and I slowly entered the room. Mia pulled back the covers, and we saw that Mom was facing the windows, so we maneuvered closer to see her face. When Mom looked at us, she had tears streaming down her face. She softly whispered, "I'm okay...in Jesus name." We started to cry, as she reached out both of her hands for us to hold onto.

Isabella came back upstairs after Father McCoy left. "Let Mommy rest," she said, as she motioned toward the door. "Come on. Let's go downstairs and talk."

When we got downstairs and Isabella asked us to sit down, I knew that this spiritual battle was nowhere near the end. Isabella began to inform us of what Father McCoy had told her. There was a look of concern on her face as she explained that something demonic was going on with our Mom, and that the evil spirit didn't like Father McCoy's presence.

Father McCoy had told my sister that it wasn't only him that had stopped the evil that was upon our mother. It was rather hard for him to explain, but that much he knew. Before she could finish sharing what Father McCoy had told her, Freddie and my cousin, Miles, came through the door all hyped up from the brawl.

They made it home in a cab and wasted no time bragging about the individual battles and chaos that were still going on. They told us that there were still fights between Bowery side and Metropolitan Avenue crew going on in certain locations throughout Bronx. As my brother and cousin were explaining what was going on, my mother called out to me, "Rock Hard!" She sounded like my mother again.

I ran back upstairs to see what she wanted.

"I have to talk to you, but first, help me up so I can go shower."

Grabbing her favorite nightgown off of a nearby chair, and her slippers from the floor, I was more than willing to help. After I got her seated, I asked, "Do you need one of the girls to help you get dressed?"

Mom was obviously still pretty weak. I turned my back to go get one of my sisters, but before I could leave she whispered, "No… I feel I can do it myself."

I went into the hallway while Mom got up and managed to get dressed on her own. She exited the room a little slower than usual with her hand pressed against the wall for balance as she walked to the bathroom. I was about to go and sit in the chair in her room, but decided not to. Instead, I went back downstairs where Freddie was still running his mouth about the rumble on Bowery Street.

"Did y'all tell Freddie what had happened to Mommy?" I interrupted.

Isabella explained what had happened to our mother,

which left both him and Miles in shock. When I mentioned that Mom was in the bathroom, the girls hurried upstairs to check on her.

When Mom finished bathing and came out of the bathroom, my sisters helped her walk back into her room to settle in. My brother, cousin, and I shared a few more stories about the battle on Bowery Street.

I knew my mother had a story to tell after her horrific ordeal. My sisters and I comforted Mom the best we could before any interrogation came into play. You see, we were all very impatient about finding out exactly what had happened to her, but we backed off, let her eat her supper and settle down, and forced ourselves to just wait.

"Hey everyone, step out into the hallway," I finally asked everybody, so that I could explain my game plan. "Isabella, make sure Mommy takes her asthma medication after she finishes eating. And make sure y'all keep reading scriptures over her until she's sound asleep."

"I think that's a good idea. Let her sleep." Freddie spoke softly.

My cousin, Miles, agreed. "Good idea, Rock Hard." We all went back downstairs to the living room, where we held our own little pow-wow. Big bro started it off by saying, "Seriously speaking, just what the hell happened to her, Isabella?"

"It was scary," Isabella began before explaining what horror she and Mia witnessed. "Right after Rock Hard left with everyone from the neighborhood, Mommy just asked us both to grab our Bibles and come pray for him."

I shook my head in disappointment, as she continued. "About an hour and forty minutes of Rock Hard being gone, Mommy's behavior changed drastically. She started shaking uncontrollably and tried writing something on a pad, but we didn't know what it was. Thank God, Rock Hard came home and figured it out."

We listened while Isabella filled us in on how they continued praying over Mom until she was in a position that she couldn't move out of.

"Mom's facial expression changed for the worst, and it didn't take a Rocket Scientist to know that something evil had taken possession of her. So, we just kept praying until Rock Hard came back with Father McCoy." My sister finished the story as looks of disbelief spread across Freddie's and Miles' face.

Big bro was not buying all that my sister was selling. Freddie was hard to convince in situations like this. He said, "Let's get Mom to a hospital."

I said, "Big bro, it was definitely something on a spiritual level. Just let Mom rest. I'm sure tomorrow she'll have answers to all of our questions. It's been a long day." There was an awkward silence, which I broke by saying, "Let's all get some rest."

It was a dark evening. After I said my peace, Freddie and Miles went for pizza and beer, and my sisters and I decided to go to bed. Two hard battles had been fought that day, but the war... the war was far from over.

17

Book of Job

After a good night's rest, life, as I knew it, went on. I got up at 3:30 in the morning to get ready for work, and Redd called to make sure I'd meet him on Metropolitan Avenue and Bane St. so we could make our journey to Speedway Race Track together.

I hung up, got dressed, and went upstairs to see how Mom was feeling. She happened to be awake and reading her Bible. Before I could get out a word she said, "I'm okay. You get to work. I'll speak with you afterwards."

I kissed her forehead and went back down the stairs. I then walked towards Metropolitan Avenue to meet Redd. Along the way, I questioned myself about what was going on around me. *Will there ever be a day when I won't have to look over my shoulders for an enemy? When will I have total peace in my life?"*

"God help me, please?" I mumbled out loud, as I made it to Metropolitan Avenue.

There were a few older brothers out on Ocean St. from the neighborhood. They wanted to congratulate me on a battle well fought. I made my "bones," as they put it. I gave them a handshake and kept moving. I didn't want to be late for work.

Redd was already on Bane St. when I had arrived. We started our daily walk to work. "Maaaan," Redd said, "Do you know how big this thing really is?"

"Not really, but I know that by the time we reach Gate 6, you'll tell me."

"Rock Hard, the cops were roaming through both neighborhoods all evening yesterday. Just what the hell happened on Bowery Street?"

"Redd, you wouldn't believe me if I told you."

He started laughing and replied, "Just tell me already." During our stroll down Metropolitan Avenue and up Jerusalem Turnpike towards Gate #6, I told it all. At one point, Redd stopped me in my tracks, looked me dead in my eyes, and excitedly said, "You're my Motha Fuckin' hero!" He had me laughing until my stomach was hurting. If anyone could make me laugh, it was definitely him, and that was what I needed most right then. *Maybe today is a good day, after all,"* I thought.

After Redd and I had walked five horses each, I couldn't wait to get home. Just as it was that morning, we walked and exchanged thoughts. It was very therapeutic because no one outside of Mother knew me better than Redd. He understood me when it came to spiritual issues, but when I explained what had happened to my mother, it left him lost for words. By the time we reached Metropolitan Avenue and Bane St., he'd heard the entire story.

Redd embraced me with a tight hug. "I love you, my brother. Stay up, and Rock Hard, be careful. You know the streets don't love anyone."

"I will my dude. You do the same." I replied, and continued on to my house.

I opened the door and just stood there wondering, *Is everything going to be all right?*

My mother yelled from her room, "Everything is going to be just fine, Swithun!"

What a wonderful gift God has given her," I thought, as I stood there with my hands on my hips shaking my head in wonder.

"Come, Swithun!" She called, in a voice full of energy. After hearing such strong words, I felt relieved that she seemed to be okay. Her voice echoed a sweet melody in my ears, as I rushed upstairs with no worries.

"Come in here before you take a shower," Mom said as I reached the top step.

I entered her room with a smile on my face, and went to sit on the bed next to her. She stopped me, "Oh, No! Don't sit on my bed smelling like them horses."

We both laughed. I sat on an old wooden chair that she had in the corner of her room next to the window. She began to explain what had transpired the previous evening. "I sent my Guardian Angel with you and your brother to help fight, and by doing so, I let my guard down." She started with a somber tone that demanded my attention. "And when that happened, your wicked grandmother had a better window of opportunity for an attack on me spiritually. I should have better prepared myself."

"But Mom, how would you have pulled that off ?"

"There are some simple spiritual remedies I could have bought before you went into such a battle."

"Like what, Mom?" I eased to the edge of the chair to clearly hear everything she had to say.

"Well, there's a store on Bowery Street right before Sutphin Boulevard, that sells prayer candles and incense. If I had Frankincense and Myrrh Granular incense and some Sage to burn ahead of time she wouldn't have been able to send anything into this house. But when I get a chance I'll send you to a friend of mine to pick up some things you should know about for any situation in the future."

I had to ask, "What exactly is Frankincense & Myrrh Granular?"

"One of the gifts the three wise men gave baby Jesus. It's used to bless a dwelling such as a Catholic Church, or your home, business, and so on."

"In other words, Mom, there are other little weapons besides good old fashion ammonia, when it comes to chasing the enemy and his foot soldiers away?"

"Why, yes Swithun! And Sage is one of them, by far. Evil spirits don't like Sage when it's being burned. They flee from it while trying to dwell in a place. But demon possession is in a whole different ballpark. If we didn't have the Angels God granted us, our battles would be a lot more challenging. Not to get off the subject, but your sister just got accepted into the Police Academy." Mom jumped right into another conversation in mid-story.

"Who?" I questioned.

"Mia, that's who," my mother replied.

I was actually very proud of her, despite my bad experiences with the NYPD in the past. After a long conversation with my queen and protector, I finally stood up and respectfully said, "Okay Mom, I'm taking a shower now."

"Good idea because she'll be here soon, so I'll let her in." Mom spoke to my back, as I left the room.

I didn't even bother to ask how she knew that Fabiana was on her way. I wanted to wash the funk off of me *ASAP*. While in the bathroom, a feeling of Fabiana and excitement overwhelmed me at the thought of her arms embracing my aching body. The last twenty-four hours had taken their toll on me. Once I finished taking a shower and spraying on some of my lady's favorite cologne, I hurried downstairs to the basement.

Fabiana was sitting on the edge of the bed with her back to me, watching TV. I crept up behind her, slid her beautiful, long, coffee-brown hair to the side, and gave her a gentle kiss on the back of her neck. It was a weak spot for her.

"Oh, no baby, not there. Stop. How was your day silly?"

"I'll show you how," I responded. I couldn't resist caressing the side of her neck with gentle kisses. She started giggling and trying to fight me off as the sweet scent of freshness wafted up my nose and sent my mind into the gutter.

"Stop, Rock Hard!" She whispered forcefully. "We have to talk. Seriously. Stop."

I took a seat next to her on the bed. I held her hand while she explained how things were not too hot at home, primarily because we were a young couple expecting a child. I tried to reason with her, but the tears started streaming down her pretty cheeks.

I placed my arm around her and pulled her close. Looking to bring some comfort to her heartache, I whispered, "Baby, stop crying. Everything is going to be all right, I promise you, love. I'll do whatever it takes to provide for you and our child."

"You don't understand. My parents are very strict. My mother keeps arguing with my father, and he's getting on me about you," She sobbed.

A piece of soul left my body, and her words put me on the defensive. "Oh yeah, what exactly is being said about me? I'm working, and at least I have a basement apartment."

"Well, in their eyes, it's not enough. We don't even have a car."

Fabiana's rebuttal touched me deeply. "Baby, I'll get another job, don't you worry. Not to mention, Fabiana, you'll be eighteen in a few months. You'll be old enough to make your own decisions. I know you're under a lot of pressure, sweetie, but I assure you, I won't jump ship."

I gently placed my right hand under her chin, lifting her head, and forcing her to look at me. I was doing my best to comfort her, while wiping the tears from her face. Fabiana's parents were stressing her out which I knew couldn't be good for our unborn child.

So, without thinking, I did the only thing a man like myself could do. I suggested that she move in with me and my family in Long Island, which was something my mother was already planning on.

"Think about it, baby. The streets are not getting any better, and I've seen enough people run out of luck. I just want you and I to live like regular people for a change, whatever that might be." I studied her expression for a moment, and went on, "Listen, baby, I know this much- I love you, and the life that I want for us and our unborn child is not here in Bronx. But listen, don't be stressing yourself out. We have some time to think things over, so in the meantime, I'll start looking for another job."

Fabiana looked beautiful even when she was crying. I couldn't help but to kiss her pretty pink lips. I threw both arms around her, and she did the same. I could feel her heart beating while we embraced, and the moment called for nothing less than a passionate kiss. It was an emotional moment that merged our souls into one.

The kiss led to her coming out of her clothes, my robe being tossed across the room, and a lovemaking session that was beyond belief. We were both stress-free by the time we got dressed, and decided to go get something to eat.

We held hands on our way to the Chinese restaurant on Metropolitan Avenue, and back to my house. Fabiana and I shared the rest of the evening down in my man cave, watching the latest hip-hop music videos on Yo! MTV Rap.

My baby loved the female rap group Salt-N-Pepper, especially their hit song back then, "Push It." She actually shared the same profile as Salt, to a degree. They had the same complexion, along with some similar facial features. Both of them wore their hair in that popular 80's do, and let's not forget those large gold bamboo earrings that most girls were wearing back then.

Fabiana might not have been a Rap Star, but she was my little superstar by far. I had always loved her and that beautiful heart that God had blessed her with. For the next couple of days following that afternoon, I went deeper into thoughts about my future. By the end of the week, the stress of the street shenanigans had taken their toll on me. I needed to relieve some tension, so that Saturday night I was in party mode. A plan to hit the Latin Quarters, my favorite spot in Manhattan, was on my agenda. I wanted to have a really good time, so I recruited some of Metro Boys' finest to roll out with me to help blow off some steam.

That Saturday evening, about twenty of us met on Metropolitan Avenue and Bane St., dressed in our best. Most of us wore black or gray leather pants, with leather Bombers or shearling coats, and Adidas. We tossed back a couple of forty-ouncers of Olde English, and some Brass Monkey as we pulled over a few dollar cabbies. The dollar cabbies mostly ran up and down Metropolitan Avenue transporting people from one end to the other for just a buck.

The driver didn't refuse the generous fare that we offered for the forty-minute ride to Manhattan from Metropolitan. We ended up piling into at least four cars that followed one another. As expected, the line-up at the Latin Quarters wrapped around the corner.

Latin Quarters maximum capacity was roughly around five hundred, but the numbers far exceeded that most weekends. The place was elbow to elbow with a mixed crowd of Blacks and Whites, but mainly Hispanics. People traveled from all parts of New York City—Brooklyn, Staten Island, Queens, New York, and even the Bronx—to party here. All five boroughs were represented, and it didn't matter if you came from a neighborhood plagued with violence.

The group of people that gathered at Latin Quarters during the early 80's had a chance to see another side of life, one other than their crack-riddled neighborhoods. This place offered a slice of life that was colored with good music and a mix of cultures—truly defining New York as a melting pot.

While waiting in the line-up on that cold winter evening, my crew got to pick and choose from all the beautiful ladies, even before getting through the door. Once inside, we lined up at the bar. The laws were not as strict back then when it came to teens drinking. In fact, we had been drinking since we left Metropolitan Avenue.

I remember being a bit of a fiend for "Brass Monkey," a cocktail recipe of juice and a couple of alcohol beverages. It was also a hit record by the Beastie Boys, hip-hop's first Caucasian group signed to Def Jams Records.

As most of our crew cleared the bar, we formed what we called "Voltron," and pretty much took over the stage area. The DJ was playing Information-Society, a Group that had a hit record called "Running," at the time. We watched the crowd dancing to the freestyle music as we sipped our drinks. We felt we could not have picked a better place to be once the next song came on.

It was almost as if the DJ knew that a large group from Metropolitan Avenue was there when he played Run-DMC's song, "Peter Piper." We broke fool on that stage as the lyrics screamed, *"Now Peter Piper picked peppers, but Run rock rhymes…!"* We danced in a circular formation, cheering, *"GO! GO! GO!"* Each of us took turns in the middle of the circle to show off our own Break Dancing routine, while the others danced around us for a few seconds, and then turned the floor over to the next homeboy.

The whole club had eyes on us because we were something to see. Our moves were well-practiced, well-choreographed, and spectacular. We were given that respect as the Metro Boys from Bronx. We spent the night dancing, socializing, and some of us were even romancing until the club shut down at four in the morning.

I don't know about the rest of the crew, but coming out of the Latin Quarters and traveling by a yellow cab back to Bronx with splendid streaks of sunrise creeping through the Manhattan skyline had me feeling like a vampire. Only God himself could create the other-worldly, picturesque view that we saw as we crossed the 59th St. bridge. It was as if a Divine Breath of Calm, passed over all that was, as if a storm passed me, and was long gone.

Unfortunately, by the time we reached Metropolitan, my stark, dark reality had returned. Running late, I asked the cab driver to wait for me, while I hurried into my house to change into some work clothing. I gave him a few extra dollars on top of what it had cost to get to the Speedway Race Track. I was about ten minutes late.

Redd was happy to see me, despite having had to walk to work alone. Truth be told, I was still a little tipsy and chewing on two sticks of Big Red gum to kill what we called the "Dragon." But, after walking a couple of horses, I had pretty much sweat out any remaining alcohol.

After my shift was over, I was too exhausted for anything. I let Redd in on my little drunken secret, and we decided to break our routine. Instead of walking home, we caught the BX2 bus. After boarding the bus, we started to have a conversation, and the next thing I knew he was waking me up as the bus reached my block. It was damn decent of him to take a ride with me to Voice St.

"You might as well come and say hello to Mom," I told him. And so he did.

My mother was downstairs hanging out in the living room. She was happy to see Redd because she knew that he and I were close friends. That was nice and everything, but the delicious aroma of maple flavored sausages had most of my attention. Mom had made us some breakfast, and more than enough to go around.

Nobody, but NOBODY could top my mother's homemade grits. She had also cooked up some scrambled eggs with cheddar cheese. All of these wonderful smells got my stomach growling so I hurried through the shower to clean up before eating. Redd was already digging into this banquet when I finally sat down at the table.

Redd and I had a brief discussion about me becoming a father and my need to seek out new employment. I needed more money in order to make a better living. My unborn child and my lady, Fabiana, were going to be my responsibility, and that was something that I didn't take lightly. I relayed to Redd the heat she was taking from her parents. I had to do something *soon*.

"What do you have in mind?" Redd asked with a mouthful of grits.

"Not sure, but I will not go back to the streets under any circumstances."

After a hearty breakfast, it was time for Redd to hit the road. Before he left, I thanked him for looking after me on the bus, and then I issued another sincere thank you to Mom for the delicious breakfast, before going to bed.

It was 11:30AM when I crashed, and approaching 10:00PM when the sound of thumping rock music forced my eyes open. My brother, Amell, was a huge fan of U2, specifically the *Joshua Tree* album. I liked a few of their songs like "Bullet the Blue Sky," and "Where the Streets Have No Name."

Once I knocked the cold out of my eyes, Amell informed me that Blue-Eyed Bully and some of the Bowery Boys had ridden through Metropolitan Avenue shooting earlier in the evening. I thought, *This is never going to end.* "Yo A, did anyone get hit?"

"Yeah, I think it was one of Brody or Pimp boys on the corner of Heart St."

"Yo, stay clear of what's going on in the streets."

"*What?* We should get after them each and every time

they do a drive-by, or attack anyone from the neighborhood," Amell argued.

"Come on bro. If that's the case this shit will never end. I have a child on the way, and my biggest concern is to leave the street thuggery in my rear-view mirror." I spoke my piece then walked up the stairs, out of the basement, through the kitchen, to the dining room, and then on to the living room.

I was about to walk up the stairs when my mother yelled, "Go back to the kitchen and grab me a Ginger Ale out of the refrigerator!"

It didn't even bother me anymore that she always knew what I was *about to* do, or what I was thinking. I grabbed a soda out of the refrigerator and continued to her room.

Before I could open my mouth, she started preaching. "Have I ever taught you the *Book of Job*?"

"I don't recall, Mommy."

She stressed the point that I should learn that part of the Bible as soon as possible, that it contained information that could provide me with the knowledge and wisdom to understand what I was going through.

"I need something besides your teaching, Mom?" I questioned.

She eyeballed me. "This *is* the teaching, and it has been all along. So, pay attention Swithun Junior because most of your answers are in the Bible."

"Okay Mom, but I am a bit worried about some other things in my life right now."

"Take it up with God by keeping your faith with the Lord and you will prevail. It won't happen on your time, and you may not get what you want. For the Lord is known for giving his worshippers the things that they need. Godspeed, my son, for judgment cometh in the morning."

I wasn't as deep into the Bible as my mother, but I was on my way. After my mother's preaching, it was pretty much time for me to get back to bed so I could be ready for work the next morning. Going back to sleep was difficult, but I finally drifted off. Concerns about my lady and unborn child being hurt by this foolish boy, Kristan, from Bowery side, stayed with me all night.

18

Prayer Work

For months, my routine was pretty much the same—working and catering to Fabiana. I also did a little studying from time to time while working on my GED. But, most of all I kept my prayers up, asking for God's help in my life.

Watching my sister take pride in her NYC Police Academy uniform brought joy to my soul. She always came home with some exciting stories about what she had learned. There was always excitement in her voice while she was in training.

She talked at great length about how she would change things within the NYPD once she got on the force. One of her top goals was gaining the public's trust within the African-American communities. Like me, Mia had witnessed far too many injustices in her growing years, but she believed that she could change things for the better, and was more than eager to try.

I must admit she had me contemplating becoming an officer, but after analyzing my life, I always felt a little discouraged. I was a chronic asthmatic, and I felt that having been expelled from high school held a hammer over my head as well. Truth be told, I constantly beat myself up because of the pressure I was feeling from my lady's parents, but fought to keep a positive frame of mind.

I was thankful to even have a job and not be on the streets selling drugs. The plan was to continue working until something else came through. Admittedly, thoughts of going back to hustling on the corner always crossed my mind, but for the sake of my unborn child, I fought my demons well.

I was always the type of person who didn't swallow shame very well. If I were to get caught committing a crime, I'd rather have died trying to escape than to suffer the consequences of doing time. That said, I preferred working for a living. It felt much better, anyhow.

As time went on, Fabiana's parents grew very anxious and wanted answers as to how I was going to provide for their daughter. They eventually invited me to a sit down over at their home on the Bowery side, of all places. I would have preferred going to Medellin, Columbia than to a community in which I was their most hated rival.

Of course, I had to start carrying a gun again while navigating those familiar and dangerous waters, but love made a man do some crazy things. This wasn't a situation I could just blow off considering how strict her mother was. It was time for me to just man up.

The night came for me to meet my lady's parents and discuss my plans over dinner. I walked up to their driveway to be greeted by Fabiana's mother, and caught her off guard when I said "good evening" in Spanish. She smiled, hugged me, and kissed my cheek before welcoming me into her lovely home.

Once inside, Mrs. Miguelina observed my every move as if she was a General in the Panamanian Army. Her militant demeanor unnerved me a bit. She was one proud Panamanian, which was evident in her choice of music-Rubén Blades salsa. There was also a photo of her and her cousin, Roberto Duran Samaniego, on display.

As far as I could tell we got along just fine with Fabiana translating back and forth since I wasn't totally fluent in Spanish.

As we got more acquainted the pleasing aroma of Latin cuisine filling the air caused a ravenous appetite to unfurl in my gut. Soon, Fabiana's father, Mr. Pedro Suarez, her sister, Narcisa, and her two brothers, who I already knew from school, walked in. I was introduced to everyone and offered a glass of traditional red Spanish Sangria.

After some more conversation, and once the Sangria began to flow through my veins, I started to loosen up. By the time supper was ready, I felt like a king. I was served an appetizer of yellow Spanish rice and pinto beans. The main course was Spanish-style chicken with red sauce, onions, and Spanish olives. Ceviche, a salad made with firm-fleshed fish pickled in acidic lime juice, accompanied the delicious meal.

We had a wonderful evening laughing and sharing stories about our struggles in life. Fabiana was quite comfortable with her parents embracing me as a family member. It was a great relief for her. Just when I thought the night was over, Mrs. Miguelina pulled me onto the floor to dance.

Thank God I'd had some salsa lessons from her daughter because this was the ultimate test of the night. Although I didn't speak Spanish fluently, I was accustomed to Latin music from hanging within my Latin circles. I was hip to the sounds of some of the greatest salsa Kings—Hector Lavoe, Willie Colon, Tito Puente, and Rubén Blades. We danced for a while before switching partners, me with my lady, and her with her husband.

At evening's end, Fabiana's parents offered to drive me home, but I considered taking a cab since we had all been drinking.

"Swithun, will you go with us to Brooklyn for a family gathering?" Mrs. Miguelina asked.

"I would be delighted."

"Okay. In two weeks I'll be looking forward to picking you up." She said.

I got big hugs and kisses from my lady and her mother, and out the door I went. Grasping my gun in my coat pocket, I canvassed the entire street as I cautiously walked to the cab. Once I made it off the block without shots being fired, I felt as if a massive slab had lifted off my chest.

I made it back to Metropolitan Avenue with no problems. As soon as I stepped through the door, Mom shouted, "Swithun, come up here!" from her bedroom.

I entered her room, and she said, "Take a shower anyway, no matter how much alcohol you had to drink."

I almost asked, "How do you know?" But Mom, being so gifted, always knew everything.

After I showered, she called me back to her room. "Come here, Swithun," she said.

As always, I did as she directed.

She said, "When you are at war spiritually alcohol and drugs work in favor of the enemy. So, think about what you're doing. Now go and get some sleep before you have to get up for work."

I caught a few hours of sleep, but what Mom told me

stuck with me throughout the morning… along with a wicked hangover. I don't even recall how I made it through the workday, but I wasn't looking to drink anything with alcohol in it for a very long time.

Redd observed me the whole day, and once we got off work, I expected him to give me a mouthful. As we walked to Gate #6 he spoke to me like the father I never had. "Yo Rock Hard, I'm sorry for the intrusion on your personal thing, but do you realize those horses we're walking weigh about 1500 pounds each?" Before I could reply, he went on, "It's bad enough you came straight to work from the Latin Quarters tipsy as all hell my brother, but let's take it down a notch." Again, I tried to get a word in and he kept talking. "And now this, Rock Hard? You're getting too comfortable with the state of being a little drunk at work."

When I finally got to reply I only said, "Yeah, Dad."

I wasn't offended and neither was he. We both just laughed it off. There was never a dull moment going to and coming from work with my friend. Redd said, "Even when I'm mad at you I can't stay mad at you. Let's catch the BX2 bus rather than walk."

Oh, good. Thank God! I was dead on my feet.

After boarding the bus, I said, "I have to get back in school and get my GED."

"Rock Hard, you have a child on the way, and you need money more than anything, my brother."

"That's why I need to go back to school — so I can make more money."

"Okay, if you say so."

His stop came before I could reply. He gave me a quick high five and said, "I'll see you later, my brother."

"Yes, tomorrow morning."

When I got off at the corner of Voice St. I noticed something in the distance—a petite female cop walking on the opposite side of the street. She wore white gloves and stepped to greet some of the guys on Metropolitan Avenue. As I crossed the street, I realized that she was my sister, Mia.

She had just graduated from the Police Academy and looked fantastic in her new blue uniform. She reminded me of Jamie Lee Curtis in the movie *Blue Steel*. I felt so proud of her as I walked up on her and tapped her on the shoulder in the middle of her entertaining some of our friends.

Mia turned and gave me a firm hug. She was so happy about her accomplishment, and so was I. It was a very proud moment in our family's history. I even felt protected walking down our block. Me, the guy who was always protecting others, felt protected on the streets for the first time in a very long while.

What a tremendous impact it had on me to observe my sister walking with such pride, her head up high. Until that moment, I had never wanted to be in a uniform so badly in my life. Our neighbors on the block were greeting Mia with congratulations as we walked down the streets. The way everyone was carrying on, it was like *All Hail to the Queen*.

My mother was delighted with my sister. As we entered our home she embraced Mia and declared, "This is just the beginning of our family's success."

Most of my siblings overwhelmed Mia with hugs and kisses and congratulations. I was in a daze, pondering what my mother had said. My mind couldn't quite grasp it, maybe because I was still a bit tired from the night before coupled with a full day's work.

Some of our friends came over to congratulate my sister as well, and before we knew it, we had a house full. I was too beat to socialize with anyone, so sticking to my regular routine, I took a shower.

Afterward, Mom called me into her room. "Alcohol is spirits, and when you are intoxicated, you open a door for trouble."

"Mom..."

"Here's something you don't know about. In case you get weak, remember that ancient Greek word, Pharmakeia, which means a pharmacy, and equates to witch or witchcraft."

I f inally got a word in. "Mom, why are you telling me this?"

"Everything has its reasons. Now go eat something and get some rest. One other thing, Swithun," she added before I made it to the stairs. "You're going to receive some excellent news this week."

For the rest of the week, I kept a cool head at work and stayed focused by keeping up some daily prayers. One day after work I told Redd not to wait for me, and decided to go to the security office to inquire about a job.

Once I reached the entrance to the security force of Speedway Race Track, I felt driven by something inside of me to move forward. There was an officer at the front desk who asked me, "Can I help you with something?"

"I'm here to apply for a security position."

"Have a seat." He walked into another office in the back where I overheard him speaking to someone whom I presumed was his superior. A moment later he returned to lead me back to Major Kelly Williams' off ice.

"Good morning, young man. I am Major Kelly Williams. How can I help you?"

"Sir, I need a better paying job. My girlfriend and I recently became pregnant with our first child. I'm a bit desperate at the moment. Also, I don't have a high school diploma, but I'm looking to take classes for my GED."

The Major looked me up and down. "How long have you been working the backstretch with the horses?"

"For three years now."

"Have you ever been arrested?"

By the grace of God, no I thought to myself. "No, sir, I haven't."

He nodded and called for the officer up front. As his employee walked back towards us, the Major commanded, "Get this young man an application and fingerprint him ASAP!" Grinning, I filled out the application and happily allowed him to fingerprint me.

Major Williams said, "It'll take a few days for your prints to come back, and then we'll see about giving you a shot, young man."

I answered, "Thank you for your time. I would greatly appreciate it if you bring me on board. You won't regret it."

"It's a bit of a process, but in due time, we'll see."

"Okay, sir. Bye for now," I replied, as the major shook my hand.

"Good day, young man."

As I made my way back down a path leading to the backstretch with the horse stables, I thought, *Did I just do what I think I did? Because, if so, it didn't feel like me at all.*

As I walked down Jerusalem Turnpike in Brooklyn County to catch the BX2 bus, something told me not to tell anyone about my semi-interview with the Major.

Once at home, I went straight upstairs to see what Mom was up to. She was actually rather chipper.

"Hey, my boy! I told you you would get some good news." And before I could get a word out, she added, "And there is more to come."

"I didn't get the job yet."

"You still have doubts, do you?" My mother started preaching, "Swithun, people fear what they don't understand. You have a little extra around you, son. Start recognizing it by prayer and meditation."

"Okay, Mom, but what's your point?"

"Well, you didn't have the mind to do what you did today. I know that much because I felt driven by something. Good fortune is coming your way, but remember what I told you about drugs and alcohol."

"Mommy, why are you telling me this for the second time?"

"No loss. Just stay clear of all bad elements, Swithun. Do what I tell you, okay?"

"All right, Mommy."

"Now go open the door for Fabiana, and don't forget to take a shower, horseman."

I couldn't help but laugh as I went down the stairs to the front door. What a God-given gift my mother had.

When I opened the front door, my love was walking away from the cab. We smiled uncontrollably at the sight of each other.

"How did you know I was coming?" My baby asked.

"Give me a kiss first, and just maybe I'll tell you."

After kissing and hugging my lady and unborn child, I held her hand and we walked into the house.

"How do you like my parents so far?" Fabiana asked.

"Very good people," I replied. "What they said about me is the big question."

"They actually like you, Rock Hard. That's a lot coming from my mother, who is skeptical of all strangers."

"So how do you feel about all that's taking place, sweetie? I mean it has to be a bit of a load off you, baby girl."

"Yeah, for now, but I know my mother. We need to get some money and get our own place."

My lady was right. We needed our own place, but getting a better paying job had to come first. Although my mother could foresee things, I wanted my new job to be a surprise once it came through. I also considered moving out of Bronx to Long Island. But one thing at a time, I reminded myself, because patience was a virtue.

My mother came downstairs to say hi to Fabiana because she was now approaching her seventh month. I told my love that after I took a shower I'd go to the store and get us some hero sandwiches.

Fabiana and Mom sat in the living room talking while I showered. Afterward, I walked back downstairs and was grateful to be greeted by the pleasant vibe passing between my two favorite ladies. Mom was telling stories about how I gave my oldest brother all kinds of problems when she'd go away with Jacob. She told how I didn't listen to his orders, and how I'd jump off the roof onto the hood of her car.

Laughing, Fabiana speculated, "I wonder if our child will be like that?"

"Not if I can help it," I said. "Okay, before y' all continue laughing at me, place your orders and tell me what kind of hero sandwiches you guys want."

After taking their orders, I said, "I already know what everyone drinks."

"Okay, take your time." Mom said.

I headed down to Holly's Deli on the corner of Cross Over St. and Metropolitan Avenue. They were known for their delicious hero sandwiches and salads. Roy, Ms. Holly's youngest son, was dragging out a big black garbage bag as I approached the store. He was a young fella sitting behind the counter the last time I visited the deli, but still recognized me.

"Hey, Roy." I said as I pushed the door open.

"Good afternoon, Mr. Rock Hard." He responded and kept on moving. I went inside, letting the door swing shut behind me.

Ms. Holly looked as if she'd seen a ghost. "Oh, my God! Where have you been? It's been a while!"

Exchanging a hug, I answered, "I've been working, and I have a child on the way."

"Really? By that pretty Spanish girl I've seen you with?"

"Why yes, ma'am," I beamed.

"How soon, Rock Hard?"

"About two and a half months from now."

"Well, Congratulations! Now, what would you like from our new menu?"

I made things easy for both of us and just handed her the list I had written. While she prepared the sandwiches, I wandered over to pick up some drinks. I asked Mrs. Holly to throw in a half pound of potato salad and some coleslaw, and once everything was prepared, I said goodbye.

"Don't be such a stranger," She said, as I grabbed the bag of food.

"Okay, I won't, ma'am. Take care."

When I returned home, Fabiana and my mother were talking about the good old days. After I handed them their lunches, Mom took hers upstairs, and Fabiana and I went downstairs to Amell's and my man cave. We finally got to eat, and enjoyed each others company for the rest of the afternoon.

I couldn't help but notice that my sweetheart was glowing brightly, and seemingly from within. She was finally at peace with me, my family, and hers. All I needed to put the icing on the cake was for that security job at the race track to come through.

Tears for Fears was playing when I put on the radio. I said, "Everybody Wants to Rule the World."

Fabiana asked, "Baby, why do you like white people's music?"

"Let me tell you something, sweetie. I am a multicultural person by nature, and I love everyone. It's only when someone tries to take advantage of others that I react. *The Bible* says, 'Do not deal treacherously without a cause.' I can't say all the sins I've committed were justifiable, but me defending others, including you and my family, I believe puts a smile on God's face. I'm not the holiest person in the church, but by God, I will repent my sins. It's simply because I was bred that way by my first leader upon this earth, my mother."

Fabiana remarked, sarcastically, "Well, okay."

"It's kind of like you with the group Salt-N-Pepa."

"Now that's different because Salt looks like me."

"Okay, baby, you win," I replied, as I went upstairs to use the bathroom.

Up there, I heard my mother's voice, "When you're done using the restroom, come here. I'd like to tell you something real quick."

Hopefully it's nothing negative. Everything has been looking up, I thought. After using the bathroom, I headed straight to Mom's room.

"It's nothing that serious." Mom stated as I entered her room with a look of concern on my face.

"What's up, Mom?"

"Did you know the Kent's that live down the block found a tombstone while digging a hole for their new swimming pool? So did Cee Cee across the street. She was digging to make a garden of flowers."

I stormed out of her room, thinking about my lady and unborn child downstairs in that creepy basement with its dark, morbid history, by herself. I had flashbacks of my Dad firing shots at a ghost that ran through the wall and the three dogs that had barked at that same wall and scratched at it until their paws bled. We hadn't had any paranormal events in a while, but I was still on edge.

I raced into the basement only to startle Fabiana with the look I had on my face. She could tell immediately that something was wrong.

"Baby, what's the matter with you?"

I just stood in the middle of the basement, glaring at the wall. I finally replied, "Nothing, Mama. Everything is okay."

I sat on the bed next to her and asked, "Whenever you stay over, I don't want you staying in the basement when I'm not here."

"Why is that?"

"Please baby just trust me on this. Either go upstairs and sleep on the couch or go up to my mother's room."

"Yes, baby, no problem."

"Rock Hard! Pick up the phone in the kitchen!" My mother yelled from the top of the stairs.

I reluctantly ran up the stairs to get the phone. It was Major Kelly Williams, from Speedway Race Track's security. "Hello, sir. How was your day, so far?" I asked.

"Not bad Swithun," he replied. "Your fingerprints came back clean young man. Can you make it into my off ice tomorrow?"

"Why, yes sir! Thank you! Is about 11:00 a.m. okay?"

"That's fine. I know you have to work at the horse stables."

"I'll see you afterward, Major Williams, and thanks again," I said before returning to the basement. I didn't want to get my hopes up high, so when my lady asked who was on the phone, I responded, "It was my boss."

"What would a horse trainer be calling you for this late in the afternoon?"

"He wants me to work a race tomorrow afternoon."

Fabiana was a bit skeptical, but I was not going to ruin the surprise by telling her the truth. The night came and went, and before I knew it I was on my way to work the next morning, praying for a much-needed blessing.

19

Trip To The Morgue

As Redd and I were on our journey to the stables I said, "Redd, with the grace of God I might be leaving J. Clinton Hawthorne racing stable soon."

"Me, too. My father has taken on some new contracts in the construction business and needs my help. This is going to be my last week."

"My brother, it sounds like we're both moving on to bigger and better things, huh Redd?"

"You know it, my dude."

"Change is good, Redd. And us getting out of this neighborhood is even better."

"I'm a part of Bronx that can't be displaced."

"I feel you, my brother, but my life circumstances have me feeling that way." Who would have ever thought back at the beginning of the summer of 1988 that this would be my last summer walking horses for J. Clinton Hawthorne? I'd been walking horses for him for three years, but I needed and wanted more.

After work, I headed over to the main security office. Major Kelly Williams came from the back office and waved for me to come in.

I politely greeted him. "Good morning, sir."

"Good morning, young man. After reviewing your application and your prints status, I decided to bring you on board."

His words nearly brought tears to my eyes. I extended my hand to shake his.

"Thank you, sir. You just changed my life."

"I am happy to do so, young man. Now let's get down to business."

Major Williams said that I would have to go through a training period. He explained that our agency secured many sectors, and then began to share some fascinating information. He followed up with the clarification "Right now, young man, I want you to understand that we are a security outfit, but we do have powers to effect an arrest. We are known as Trackdown Security and have a history that goes way back to the cowboy days. Do you like Western movies, Swithun?"

"Why, yes," I replied.

"Which Western movies have you seen, so far?" The Major wanted specifics.

"Well, *The Good, the Bad and the Ugly*" I replied, and we

both started laughing. "I've also seen *Once Upon a Time in the West*."

"Now, that's a good one, Swithun, but have you ever seen any movies about a bank and train robber by the name of Jesse Woodson James? He was an American outlaw."

"I've heard of Jesse James, but never seen a movie about him."

"Well, young man, you're about to catch up on some serious history."

Apparently, the Trackdown agency first made its name in the warrant of Jesse James and his gang, but it wasn't the Trackdown agency that killed Jesse James in 1882. It was one of his own for the bounty. I guess even back then there was no honor among thieves.

"Wow!" I said as the Major finished the history lesson.

"We are the remaining portion of the Trackdown agency."

"That's incredible."

"Now let's get you processed."

We walked to a nearby room that had tons of uniforms. After one of his staff sized me up, I was given four pairs of gray pants with dark blue stripes down the sides, and two long-sleeved shirts, as well as two short-sleeved shirts. The shirts were dark blue with a horse's head patch on the left shoulder. Above the patch was the word "Trackdown," and below it, "NYRA Security," which stood for New York Racing Association.

Major Williams had me put on a long-sleeved shirt and a gray tie for a photo to be used on my employment identification card. I was also given a gold badge that was identical to a New York Police Sgt. shield. After being fitted for a hat, I was given one that was identical to those worn by the New York State Troopers, bearing a gold shield in the front.

I was overwhelmed big time. Once my ID was laminated and given to me, the Major gave me a training manual and informed me of my start time for the next day.

My appointed sergeant's name was Audrey Baxter. I was told to report to her after roll call. Major Williams firmly shook my hand and said, "Welcome aboard, Wright, and be on time for roll call."

"Yes, sir." I saluted.

I decided to take a cab home, considering all I had to carry. I still intended to keep it a secret from my lady if she wasn't already at the house when I got there. The plan was to put my uniforms upstairs in my mother's room before anyone could see them.

When I arrived home, my baby was still there but was taking a shower, and that was perfect timing for me. I ran into my Mom's room and put my stuff in her closet. I hid everything except the training manual because I still had some reading to do. My plan was to at least get my first paycheck from Trackdown before letting Fabiana in on the good news.

To my surprise, her parents were on their way to get her for a doctor's visit. I wasn't happy about getting rid of my love for the rest of the day, but it worked in my favor. Now, I had plenty of time to study the manual, and then head out to the store for a new pair of uniform shoes and black belt to match. By the time Fabiana was out of the shower and had gotten dressed, her parents were blowing the horn in the driveway. She gave me a quick kiss and hug as she went out the door.

After showering, I got dressed and walked up the block to Dolly's Deli for a cream cheese bagel and orange juice. Afterward, I caught the BX2 bus to the Storm St. Mall.

While riding the bus, I read through part of the training manual. I couldn't believe what I was reading. Trackdown Security was not just your ordinary security firm. They had Peace Officer status, which generally referred to any employee of a State, County, or Municipality. It was somewhat like a Sheriff's department or other public law enforcement agency with its authority to arrest, perform searches, and enforce seizures.

We also had the power to execute criminal and civil warrants. I was a part of an agency that was responsible for the "prevention or detection of crime, or for the enforcement of certain dwellings". If this wasn't a step up in life, I didn't know what would be. My spirits were up, and I was feeling amazingly blessed by God.

Shopping was simple since the store I shopped at had both items. I was in and out and back to the bus terminal, and all without a fight. I didn't see any of my enemies, nor was I worried about any of them. I made my way back to the BX2 and went home. Mom was already there.

Just as soon as I made it inside she shouted from her room, "What did I tell you about receiving good fortune!"

I replied as I jogged up the stairs, "Yes, Mom, you did say so. I didn't doubt you. It's just that a lot is being thrown at me all at once."

"There's more to come, my dear son." She assured me as I entered her room.

"Mom, where are the needle and thread? I have to hem my pants."

"I'll do it for you."

I spent most of the evening studying the training manual and was very focused on the need-to-know information. When my lady gave me a call, she remarked, "All of a sudden it seems like you're not yourself."

"What do you mean, sweetie? I'm the same as I've always been."

"I know you better than you know yourself. I'll be there tomorrow."

"Tomorrow I have to work a race out of town, so I won't be home in the morning, but I'll be here in the evening."

"In that case I'll be over the following day." she said. As I hung up the phone, I sighed and said to myself, "That was close."

The next morning, Mom lit up at the sight of me in my uniform. "I thank God for giving birth to such a handsome man. Now let's get you to work. It is always good to be early." She grabbed the car keys off her nightstand, and we left the house together.

We slid into her reliable old Cadillac, and away we went. While driving, she said, "You are really playing this thing out, huh?"

"Playing what out, Mommy?"

"Don't get smart with me because you're in uniform. You know what I'm talking about."

I flashed her a smile. "Yes, Mom. It's just not the right time to tell her. I will when I get around to it."

"Okay, son. I didn't mean to push so hard."

"It's okay, Mommy...love you. Remember, we're not going to Gate #6. I'm working in the grandstand area now, not the backstretch where the horses are, so it will be the gate where Security is directing traffic."

"I saw them as we drove up to the entrance." she replied as we entered the vast parking lot to Speedway Race Track.

Two clean-cut Caucasian officers were out there controlling traffic and Mom asked for directions to roll call. Noticing my uniform, they both greeted me. "Welcome aboard! Someone must like you to have placed you in our patrol division."

"Why do you say that?" I questioned.

"Because SSW division has a bit of a shit job guarding the horses at night." The shorter of the two officers responded and directed us toward the right place.

Before I slid out of the car, Mom pointed upward. "Somebody up there is looking out for you."

"Don't I know it."

As I walked away from the car toward the entrance, she shouted, "Have a good day, Rock Hard!"

I arrived a little early and met some of the younger officers, who were pretty cool. Some of the older ones were a bit standoffish and not too friendly, but I came to work not to make friends.

Soon, many more officers reported for duty, as well as our Supervisors. There was a Captain, Lieutenant, and Sergeant. We lined up in five rows of ten across, and the captain gave a speech on what to do if an elder suffered a heat stroke.

Some quarters held cold water, and we were told to apply it to ankles, under the armpits, and to the neck to help revive them until they could be given proper medical attention. A few of us new guys were also shown where the first aid equipment was located in case we needed it.

Right after roll call, I reported to Sgt. Audrey Baxter, a tall, Caucasian woman with salt and pepper hair and a tough demeanor. I followed her toward a staircase and she informed me of what I'd be doing throughout the day. "You're going to be working the second-floor grandstand area where we guard the betting bays and perform a few other assignments."

There were about five bays spaced out through the grandstand area. Sgt. Baxter brought me over to the one I would be guarding and introduced me to the staff running it.

"If one of these lights go on over these windows to the betting bays, you are to walk over and investigate the matter." they explained.

That was my first assignment. Four or five other officers and I positioned ourselves between the stands and the grandstand floor facing the bays, watching for any signs of trouble. I paced back and forth within my little sector, anticipating something going wrong.

As the day went on, the crowd grew. It was time to become more vigilant. I couldn't help but notice that only Sgt. Baxter and one other officer carried firearms. The rest of us had whistles to blow if we needed assistance.

After a couple of races, Metropolitan Avenue's very own Mr. Steve Williams a.k.a. Fun, from the Rap group Two Mic's, showed up. He was a bit surprised to see me working there, considering he knew me as more of a roughneck. I could tell that seeing me in uniform threw him off a little.

Nevertheless, he was happy for me and gave me a homeboy hug. "Congratulations. You are always doing something good, Rock Hard. I'm proud of you! This is the guy I prefer you to be. God bless you, my brother, and keep up the good work."

Steve was a God-fearing man, as he came from good folks. When he said something, he meant it soulfully.

Shortly after my conversation with Fun, my Sgt. relieved me for my lunch break. Before letting me go, she simply stated, "You're new Swithun, so I won't hold it against you, but we are only to socialize for business, okay?"

"Yes, ma'am." I answered in full understanding.

"Now run along. You have an hour of lunch. Be back on time."

"Yes, ma'am, I will," I replied.

I went for a little bit of a walk and stopped by a hot dog stand where I met Gino, a young man like myself. He was hard-working and operated a concession stand. After striking a conversation with him, I decided that he was a really cool Italian brother.

"There is a lot of money on this fucking track, Swithun, but you got to make money to buy a ticket." Gino stated, and then paused to address someone walking by. "Hey ya, doll!" I turned to see who he was talking to, and it happened to be a woman in her sixties. When I turned back to him, he said, "Eighteen to eighty, blind, crippled and crazy!"

I laughed so hard I nearly dropped my pretzel and soda. "Enough knowledge from you for one day. See you later." I said, while slowly straying away.

On my way back to the grandstand, I was stopped by Sgt. Big John. "Are you new, young man? Because I don't believe I've seen you before."

"Why, yes, sir, I am."

"Did you make your roll call this morning?"

"Yes, sir!"

"That means you started at 10 am. Young man, how would you like to do some overtime this evening?"

"Why, yes, sir, it would be a pleasure."

He demanded my name and radioed to Sgt. Baxter to

inform her of my delay. He then ordered me to report to a Lieutenant by the name of Anthony Lukes right after my shift.

Shortly after my discussion with Sgt. Big John, I ran to a nearby phone booth to place a call home and let my mother know I'd be working until 2 am. Mom was out at that moment, but my brother Amell was there, so I relayed the message to him. I hurried back to my post to relieve Sgt. Baxter.

"I see you are making friends pretty fast. And, if you're a bit of a yes-man when it comes to overtime, you will be well-liked."

"Thanks for the advice, Sgt. Baxter. I'm eager to work, and I really do appreciate the job."

"With that attitude, you'll do just fine. Now, don't forget to report to Lieutenant Lukes at eighteen hundred hours."

"Sgt. Baxter, Sgt. Big John said to meet him at 6:00 pm."

"It's Sgt. John Houch. And if you're going to continue working here, it's a must that you learn military time."

"Yes, ma'am."

"And for the record, eighteen hundred hours is 6:00 pm, in military time."

"Thanks again, ma'am."

"Carry on," she replied and walked over to the next betting bay to relieve another officer for his break.

The rest of my shift was as smooth as butter, and before I knew it, it was time to go and meet the Lieutenant. When I arrived at the office, Lieutenant Lukes was waiting for me. We greeted each other, and he gave me my assignment.

I was given a flashlight and a clock with an old fashion keyhole in it. Lieutenant Lukes explained what I would be doing for the rest of the evening. "I will walk you through the first round, and then you're on your own. There are several locations that have a key you will be placing into this clock and turning twice each time. It will show when you were last in that location. You will have about fifteen minutes of downtime in between each round. Also, you have an hour break starting at twenty-two-hundred hours. When you're making your rounds, you'll be looking for the obvious such as fire, and anyone unauthorized moving about."

Huh? Unauthorized?

Seeming to read my expression, he clarified, "That only means anyone out of a uniform. Check them out."

"Yes, sir."

My new assignment was actually better than the first one because it involved movement and some downtime. When it was time for my break, I was approached by an officer instead of a supervisor. He introduced himself as Tony Caraballo. He told me that if I went up to the clubhouse there would be something to eat and drink. Afterward, he gave me directions to a staircase that would lead me there. "And oh, if you would like to take a nap afterward, come see me."

"Okay, my friend," I replied. "And thanks for the professional courtesy."

As I began walking, I said to myself, "This gig is too good to be true."

Walking into the clubhouse was like crossing the threshold into a different world. About fifteen guards were lounging around, eating, and drinking beer and other alcoholic beverages, while in uniform. It was definitely a culture shock for me, but what caused my heart to sink was the sight of an officer sniffing cocaine through a dollar bill.

At that point, I decided that a nap sounded better. I went looking for Tony, who led me to an area beneath the grandstands. He said, "These beds down here are pretty comfortable."

As we walked further into this huge room, I noticed a series of box-shaped doors lining the wall. I had to ask, "Tony, what is this place?"

He replied, with a nonchalant flick of his hand, "Oh, it's a medical facility—and a morgue for the deceased of the race track community."

A fucking morgue? Are you kidding me? Dead people had been visiting my house all of my damn life, and just like my mother, I saw them. I woke up fast and hard as if I were hit by a bucket of ice water. He wanted me to take a nap in a place where dead people were stored away in refrigerators.

Tony had no way of knowing that I had a sensitivity to the world of spirits, and I wasn't about to tell him. I kept that stuff to myself. Shortly after he left, I was out of there. Nobody was happier than I was when my shift ended.

I was about to call a cab when I realized that my mother was waiting outside the gate. Mom was kind of used to being up in the middle of the night reading her Bible, so it wasn't a big deal for her to come and get me.

Once I got into the car I said, "You're too much. You should be sleeping."

"So, how did it go?"

"Well, Mom, I witnessed first-hand what you were warning me about as far as drugs and alcohol, but after thinking about life in general, I'm doing pretty well."

We were approaching a red light on Jerusalem Turnpike, and my mother glared at me with a look that could kill. "Why are you feeling that way, Swithun?"

"Well, I have a new job with decent pay, and on top of

that, I have the same powers as the police officers. Not to mention, the love of my life is about to give birth. It feels like something spiritual broke from around me, Mommy. Things are so clear right now."

"Have you read the Book of Job in the *Holy Bible*?" Before I could answer, she said, "I know you didn't."

"No, Mom, I didn't get around to it yet, but I'm telling you, we won some kind of battle. I can feel it, Mommy." I enthusiastically responded.

With a serious expression and a somber tone, she whispered, "No son... it would take you reading the *Book of Job* to realize that this is just the beginning of the fight for your soul."

20

The Messenger

The streetlight turned green, and Mother slowly pulled off, leaving me in deep thought. *What deep battles were coming next?* Once we got home, I went straight downstairs to undress before showering. After I showered, Mom called me to her bedroom.

"Swithun, can you please start reading the *Book of Job*? Read a little at a time." Mother said as I entered the room.

"Of course, Mom. I will. Good night. And I love you for your teaching." I concluded, before kissing my Queen gently on her forehead and exiting the room.

Once back in the basement, I grabbed my *Bible*, sat on the edge of my bed, and read a couple of pages of the *Book of Job* before going to sleep. At first, I was a bit confused. Job's struggles were utterly different than mine.

Job 1:13 had my mind baffled after reading the part about his sons and daughter eating and drinking at the oldest brother's house. That could not have been my oldest brother, Freddie. It would only be a dream because I had seen this guy in action when it came to food.

Also, I wasn't trying to contradict sin, but in modern times, it was a bit off the hook. The enemy and his foot soldiers had run rampant in their search for souls. Maybe it had always been that way.

At around 3:00 am I decided to call it a night. Roll call was at 10:00 and I desperately needed sleep, so it only took minutes to doze off.

Once asleep, visions of a baby boy appeared in my dream. We were in a pure white room with no doors or windows, just him and I. *Whose child is this?* I wondered when I first saw the handsome little white fella. He couldn't have been mine, but he was a beautiful baby. I could tell he was happy as his arms and legs flailed with joy, and this sense of bliss radiated into and through me.

The loud ringing sound of my alarm clock jolted me out of the dream. The digital clock displayed 8:00 am as I rubbed the cold out of my eyes. The sense of joy that I had experienced in the dream lingered within me.

Once my feet hit the ground, I couldn't help but notice my brother lying with a gorgeous Latin honey on the other side of the basement. Not that it was my business, but they were both butt naked. I quickly grabbed my uniform, along with everything I needed for the day, and hurried upstairs.

As I approached the second floor of the house, I could hear the shower running. It caught me by surprise because the bathroom was usually vacant at this hour. With my eyebrows raised, I cautiously moved toward the bathroom door and gently tapped on it.

My youngest sister, Gabriella, called out, "Yeah?"

"What the hell are you doing out of school?" I asked.

"I'm sick."

"If you don't get out of my way, you're going to be sick for real."

I could hear my mother in her bedroom, laughing, and I became mildly irritated when she directed, "Leave your sister alone, Swithun!"

"Yeah, stupid," Gabriella added her two cents.

"I wasn't stupid when I came to your rescue on Bowery Street."

"Isabella and Mia could have done that." she argued.

"Do you not know I got police powers now? Get out that damn bathroom, girl!"

"*Mommy!*" Gabriella yelled as if someone was killing her.

"Enough! Both of you!" Mother interjected, before demanding to see me.

I could hear Mom laughing until I reached her bedroom. "Mom, what's so funny?"

"Your little sisters are growing up on you." she stated before her expression became more somber. "Does Amell still have company?" I shamefully turned away as I heard Mom whispering, "It's his sin, not mine."

"Mom, she might be the one for him." I defended my younger brother.

At that moment, Gabriella finally came out of the bathroom saying, "I'm going to be a cop, just like Mia."

"For what?" I said. "When shit hits the fan, you're going to run and hide like you did with Alfonso Sancho in the Plaza Mall on Storm St."

Gabriella became unhinged, and screeched, "Mommy, tell Swithun to leave me alone!"

I fell out laughing as I walked down the hall to the

bathroom. Sidestepping her, I said, "I can see Violet and Penelope being police officers, but you better go work in a pie shop."

Mom shouted, "Boy, hurry up and take a shower so I can get your butt to the race track!"

"Alright, Mother."

Gabriella asked, "When are he and Amell moving out?"

"When you're old enough to take care of yourself." I fired back, before ducking into the bathroom.

When I was finally showered and dressed, Mom was already outside in the vehicle, beeping the horn. Before stepping out of the front door, I called out to my sister, "Gabriella, make sure you don't tell Fabiana where I'm working."

Once in the vehicle, Mother and I headed to Speedway Race Track. En route, I quietly reflected on the dream I'd had. After a while, Mom asked, "What's on your mind, Swithun?"

"I had a dream last night that was kind of weird but pleasant."

"What about?"

"I was in this pure white room, and it seemed like the walls continued forever. It didn't have any doors or windows. In the middle of it was a white bassinet that resembled a chariot with gold trimmings, and in it was a naked baby boy. He was adorable as all heck."

"So what was so weird about it?" my mother questioned, without taking her eyes off of the road.

"I thought he couldn't be mine because he was white."

Mom pulled off the road in a burst of uncontrollable laughter.

"Mom, you're going to make me late."

"You're already late upstairs in your brain." She stated while pointing to her head.

After composing herself, she pulled from the curb and continued on. We drove in silence until I finally had to ask, "What did you find so funny about my dream?"

"What nationality is Fabiana?"

"She's Panamanian and Colombian."

"What complexion is she, Swithun?" Mom quizzed me as if I was in elementary school.

"She's considered to be a white Hispanic," I replied.

"I rest my case."

"Mom, is that it?"

"Swithun, you have European traits. In case you haven't noticed, so do your brother, Alfonso, and sister, Gabriella. They have the same parents, you know. Not to mention whatever your father is mixed with, with his Spanish-looking self."

By the time our conversation ended, we were greeting the guards at the main gate. Before she dropped me off, I reminded her, "make sure to tell Violet and Penelope not to let Fabiana know about my new job."

"You didn't have to remind me. I was already thinking that."

"Alright, Mother. Love you, and see you at six. I'm not going to do any over time."

"Okay, see you later."

As I was walking to the Grandstand area for roll call, I ran into Gino. He assured me that it was okay to run up a tab every now and then as long as I squared up with him on payday. He continued rambling on and on, but the only thing I got out of it was, "What a Goomba I am, right, Swithun?"

"Yes, you are, my brother. I'll see you later, Gino." I politely brushed my new friend off to make it to roll call on time.

I was ten minutes early. The supervisors pretty much gave the same instructions as the day before. The only thing out of the norm was the presence of a new officer. He was told to hang back by one of the lieutenants. After roll call, he introduced himself as Joey Lorenz, a cool Sicilian brother from Bensonhurst Brooklyn, New York.

We had a brief conversation, and he was actually thrilled over the assignment he was given. He got to ride inside of an ambulance that followed the horses during the race.

"What did I do to deserve such a gig, Swithun?" Joey asked.

"I'm not sure, but I don't have that kind of luck. Maybe it's because you look like Sylvester Stallone." I joked. "Good luck, Joey, and enjoy your shift."

"You do the same, Swithun. See you later."

I expeditiously marched off to my post in the Grandstand area. Once there, Sgt. Baxter called me over to where she and the other officers were engaged in a briefing. Sgt. Baxter informed us that if we ever encounter a confrontational individual, we were to blow our whistles to get the attention of the other officers.

"Numbers count in most situations, so it's imperative to get the attention of your back up before things escalate, whether I'm on the floor or not. Got that, gentleman?" Sgt. Baxter concluded.

"Yes, ma'am." Every officer replied simultaneously.

"Carry on." Sgt. Baxter stated before every man took his post.

The day ran smoothly until the lunch break. Considering Fabiana was coming over to my house later, I decided against a heavy lunch. That way I could get something to eat for the both of us, or I should say, the three of us. I grabbed a bag of BBQ chips and a Pepsi and then found a bench at the opposite end of the Grandstand. I bent down to my left to sit my soda on the ground, and when I straightened up, a pleasant elderly woman was sitting beside me. I thought that was a little strange since I hadn't heard her approaching, the area wasn't crowded, and there were other places she could have chosen to sit.

Although a bit startled, I said, "Hello, ma'am. How are you?"

She responded an unusual accent, "I am doing fine, and you, young man?"

"I can't complain. Things are going pretty good."

"Ain't that the truth," she replied, "but you have a long road ahead of you."

I assumed she was referring to the fact that I was so young compared to her advanced years, but that was neither here nor there, so I let it slide. "Ma'am, I'm sorry for the intrusion on your personal thing, but you have an unusual accent. Where are you from?"

"Oh, I'm from the East," she replied.

"Oh, okay, so you're from Long Island. My family and I are moving there soon." While I spoke, I couldn't help but notice her bright white attire, and the fact that she wore no shoes. Since we were walking distance from the grassy picnic area, I concluded that her bare feet were not so unusual, after all. I continued munching on my chips.

She continued speaking while I reached down for my Pepsi. "I know where you're moving to but remember, Swithun, that you were chosen."

Chosen? What the...? I caught a glimpse of her smiling face in my peripheral vision before she vanished into thin air.

Frightened out of my mind, I jerked back from where she had been sitting. To make matters worse Sgt. Baxter chose that particular moment to walk up on me. My startled expression must have been evident because she gently patted me on the back.

"Relax, Wright. You still have twenty-six minutes left of your break. I just wanted to give you your Portable Patrol Guide with a report notebook in it. You are to make daily entries in it, such as the start of a shift, the time you take a break, and who relieves you of your duties. Also note if you get a complaint from anyone, especially betting bays' personnel. Myself, as well as some of the other supervisors, will be periodically checking them. Got that, Wright?"

I was reluctant to answer because of what had taken place prior to Sgt. Baxter walking up on me. Should I report that shit? Would anyone even believe me? No. I tossed the idea around in my head as I was still justifiably very rattled from that encounter.

The Sgt. said, "Wright, are you okay? Because you look like you saw a ghost?"

"Yes, ma'am. I'm sorry for the delay in answering you. I was pondering some yard work."

"Oh, I know the feeling. My home sits on an acre of land, and it's pretty warm out today. Anyway, Wright, enjoy your break."

"Yes, ma'am." As she walked away, I thought about how I'd rather be a normal person. This day could not be over with fast enough.

After the break, I went back to my post, and I tried to decipher what the spirit had said to me. It almost felt like a dream, but I knew it wasn't because I was here on the job, in broad daylight, wide awake. My God, what's next? I'm sorry to question Your authority, my Lord, but I know of Your existence. I recited a few Hail Mary's and Our Fathers to myself while still trying to focus on my duties.

Finally at the end of my shift, I was relieved by another officer. After getting his name and making an entry, I headed to the office to punch out. Although I didn't work a double, I sure felt like it after the encounter.

As soon as I slid into my mother's car, she knew something was bugging the heck out of me. She said, "What's wrong with you?"

I fired her a glance. "You mean *you* don't already know?"

"I'm not God, and some things are sacred between you and God. So, tell me, what happened?"

"Mom, I got a visitor today, and she was not of this world."

"What?" Mom replied. "Were you in the restroom or something?"

"No, Mommy. I was sitting on a bench during lunch break. I leaned over to my left to put my soda on the ground, and when I came up, an elderly white woman was sitting right next to me on my right."

"So what did she say, Swithun?"

"She's from the East. That's all she said. I assumed that meant she was from Long Island."

"No, son. She meant the Middle East."

"Wow!" I said. "This is too deep."

Mom pressed on. "What else did she say, son?"

"For me to remember that I was chosen…right before she disappeared."

"She is what they call a Messenger, Swithun. Consider yourself lucky."

"Mother, I was scared to death, I don't feel so lucky about that."

"You'll get used to it."

"Oh, that's reassuring, Mother dear. What do you think this visit was for?"

"I think what she's trying to say is that your battles are far from over."

"I kind of figured that because now that I'm thinking back, she also stated that I have a long road ahead of me."

"That can also mean prosperity," Mom replied.

"In what aspect of my life?"

"It can mean a long life, good luck, and being prosperous."

By now, we were only a few blocks away from home. "All right, Mom, I'd rather change the subject. Is Fabiana at the house?"

"Yes, your little butterball is there." Mom chuckled.

"What floor is she on? And did Gabriella leave the side door unlocked?"

"Yes, and she's upstairs laying across my bed, Swithun, watching television."

"Good stuff, Mom, I'll tell her soon."

"She's already very curious about the times you're getting in here."

"All I need is for you guys to stick with the plan for a few more weeks."

As we were turning onto Voice St. off of Metropolitan Avenue, Mom said, "you better hope she's not looking out of my window."

"Okay, Mommy, I have to ask. Can you see her in the window with your psychic ability?"

"I am on God's time. Get that through your thick skull."

I let out a heavy sigh. "What a heavy day."

"You better thank God for every day He sends your way. Do you understand, Swithun? That means for the good ones as well as the bad ones."

"I understand, Mother. It's just a lot to handle." I replied, while still wishing I could just be a normal guy with a normal life through which ghosts, spirits, and demons didn't traverse on their way to somewhere else.

21

Preach On

I slipped into the house by the side door to avoid running into Fabiana. I wanted to tell her about my new job at just the right time, and this new uniform would give me away before I was ready. Once inside, I moved swiftly to the basement to change. With a towel and clean underwear in my hand, I headed upstairs to take a shower. While passing the living room, I bumped into Gabriella.

"You owe me some money." She teased.

I knew she was kidding, but since she had left the side door unlocked her claim had some truth to it. I wasn't going to tell her that, though, so I headed up to the second floor. At the top of the stairs, my first impulse was to run down to Mom's room to kiss Fabiana, but then I decided that I had better not. Since she thought I was still working with horses, if I went to her before showering and didn't smell like a horse, she'd catch on.

Instead, I shouted from the hallway, "Baby, I love you, but I have to run to the bathroom."

The only response I got was the sound of Fabiana's and Mom's laughter floating down the hall. I didn't think I was funny, but oh, well, it didn't matter. I ducked into the bathroom.

After a hot shower, and with the relief that our espionage maneuvers had worked, I felt normal again. When I walked into my mother's room, my sweetheart was looking so beautiful as a pregnant woman. She had such a glow to her lovely face that I wasted no time embracing and kissing her.

"Now that's too much weight on my bed, you two." Mother joked with us, and we all got a good laugh out of that. "And don't have her going down to the basement because that's too much on her.

Mom was concerned because Fabiana was eight months pregnant already. She then suggested that we hang out in Freddie's room downstairs, which was a small room off of the living room and our indoor porch. Freddie was staying with Grandma Royce at the time in Brooklyn.

As Fabiana and I were headed to Freddie's room, I asked her, "Baby, did you eat?"

"Yes, I had pizza earlier."

"Where did you get pizza from?" I questioned.

"On Bowery Street by the bus terminal."

"Baby, you took a bus here?" I asked while turning on the radio in Freddie's room.

"Leave it there that's my song," Fabiana demanded as *Toy Soldiers*, a song by Martika, was playing.

"Fabiana, did you take the bus?" I asked again.

"Yes, Swithun...I took the bus."

"Baby, why would you do such a thing in your state?"

"I just wanted to feel free again and not be a hostage anymore." she whined with an attitude while plopping down onto the bed.

"Okay, I didn't mean to push, but I'm concerned about you and my child always. She was only half listening because she was enjoying her song *Toy Soldiers*. "Anyway, sweetie, I didn't eat earlier because I wanted to get something with you. Fabiana, you hear me?" I had to ask after she closed her eyes and began singing the song.

"Yes, baby, but let me finish my song." she said after I interrupted her groove.

"Okay. All right, Mama." I surrendered and just laid back on my brother's bed while she finished singing.

Won't you come out and play with me?
Step by step
Heart to heart
Left, right, left
We all fall down
Like toy soldiers

I got a kick out of seeing her so happy and singing with such passion. When the song went off, Fabiana gently pushed me and said, "Move over so I can take a nap."

"You're the boss," I said sarcastically. "But Fabiana, please mama take a cab next time. I don't need any of my enemies from the past approaching you or saying anything to you that would pull me back in the streets. That's not good for the three of us."

My baby turned in my direction and started kissing me with tears flowing down her face.

"Are you okay, my love?" I asked.

"Yes, as long as the three of us are together."

"Fabiana, I promise you we will be."

We held each other tight as she got comfortable and cried herself to sleep in my arms.

Mother had tip-toed to the door and waved at me to come out. Carefully extracting myself from Fabiana's arms, I crossed the room to see what she wanted.

"Yes, what's up, Mom?"

Mom stated, "her emotions are going to go from one extreme to the next, so be careful. And you told her right about taking a cab. She did run into someone you had a fight with, but they just asked how you were doing."

"Gabriella!" I shouted up the stairs.

"What?" My little sister replied.

"Watch out for Fabiana! If she wakes up tell her that Mommy and I went to get food from Al's Pizzeria."

My little sister was happy because I was going to treat everyone to some pizza. Al's up on American Avenue was by far one of the best pizza shops in Bronx, New York. They were also known for all sorts of other Italian dishes, and I mean they were top notch.

My mother gave me *the look*. "Don't let your little authority from Speedway Race Track go to your head."

"Sorry, Mom, I was going to ask you."

"Well considering I can go for a chicken Parmesan sandwich, I don't mind giving you a ride."

As we drove up the block and signaled a right-hand turn on to Metropolitan Avenue, my mother started to preach to me. "Son, have you been keeping up with your prayers?" she asked as I gazed aimlessly out the window.

"Yes, Mom, I pray," I responded while waving at some of the Metro Boys hanging out on the corner.

"I need for you to start getting deeper into your prayer."

"Okay, Mommy, I will."

"It's not just you anymore. You have a family now. Take the steps very serious when your child is born because you will carry his sins for the first thirteen years of his life. Everything you do will reflect on him whether you're there or not."

Mother's last statement grabbed me like a 300-pound Samoan wrestler and wouldn't let go. In fact, it had gotten my undivided attention.

"Mommy, why would you say whether I'm there or not?"

"Swithun, I'm just speaking hypothetically."

"Not to offend you, Mother, but it didn't sound like it."

Before she could respond, Party Boy, a cat from Metropolitan jumped in front of the car like a crazy person. My mother started to curse him out before she got a good look at him. He started hugging Mom through the window. Party Boy just happened to be one of my mother's favorite people. She was happy to see him. There we were, in the middle of the street on Bane and Metropolitan Avenue, shooting the breeze for a moment.

After Party Boy finished hugging mom he came around to my window. He gave me a hug and started punching me in a friendly fashion. "When are we going to have another war?" he asked out of the blue.

His comment had my eyebrows raised. And before I could speak, Mom shouted at him, "Now Party Boy, don't even start! Swithun is on the straight and narrow from here on out."

"I'm just kidding, Mama Wright," Party laughed.

"Okay, baby, you take care of yourself in the streets." Mom replied before we pulled off.

We went up Metropolitan Avenue and made a left onto Southern Boulevard. We cruised up to American Avenue where we made another left turn and a quick right turn into a small shopping center where Al's Pizzeria was. Mother parked in front of Al's, placed the car into park, and turned it off. "I'll wait in the car. You know what I want, Swithun, and don't forget to get me a 2-liter of Ginger Ale."

"Okay, Mama, I'll be right back."

After walking into the pizza establishment, I did a quick scan of the interior before walking to the counter and placing my order. You could never be too careful when it came to stumbling upon an enemy. For me, it became routine after some trials and tribulations in my life.

This time it happened to be quiet and the coast was clear. I was able to place my order in peace, all the while anticipating trouble. I ordered three regular pizza pies and one Sicilian pie with a large order of stuffed shells with meatballs. I also requested a large spaghetti and meatballs, and made sure not to forget about Mama's chicken parmesan.

"Okay, give me 20 minutes." said the gentleman that waited on me.

Since it was going to take a little bit, I went back to the car with mom and waited it out.

"Don't forget the sodas." Mom said as I approached the car.

"Okay, Mother, on the way out I'll get them."

"God, I hope you let the Angels near to watch over that boy." Mom blurted out.

"Mommy, who are you talking about?"

"Party Boy, that's who, Swithun! Have I ever told you about the night a bunch of gunshots went off on Ocean St.?"

"No, you haven't, Mother."

Mother began to explain to me how a few weeks earlier, shortly after midnight, she heard some loud and rapid gunshots that demanded her attention. She instinctively rushed to look out the window and saw Party Boy scurrying from the direction of the shots.

"That boy was jumping over fences. Once he got on our side of the block, he looked up at me and said, 'Hi, Mrs. Wright.' And I was so glad to see that he was not hurt. I replied 'Hi, Party Boy' and he just kept hopping fences."

"Mommy, we live in a rough neighborhood that has lots of enemies."

"Let me tell you something, Swithun. The one thing you have going for you is that you listen to me as your teacher. You made a U-turn from the Avenue of devastation, and in time will become someone decent. Not everyone has what God has put around you, Swithun, and I hurt when I witness these fatherless children in this neighborhood and what they all go through."

"I understand, Mother, but it's kind of what you told me a while back. We can't save the world."

"Yes, that is free will God has given, and because of your gift, we are aware of the battle more than others. The fact that we try to love with our whole heart we are blessed a hundredfold."

"I know that now, Mommy, from all you passed down to me, but the fact remains that this is God's battle. All we can do is serve Him and fight what's at hand."

When I turned to my mother after my last statement, she was smiling and glowing. "Preach on, brother Wright. You're getting it my son, but you have a lot more to learn. Now go and get our food and don't forget the drinks."

I went back inside Al's to get our order and drinks. I

made sure not to forget the three 2-liter sodas: Canada Dry Ginger Ale, Sunkist orange, and Coca-Cola. After grabbing our large order, I strolled back to my Mom waiting for me in the car. As I approached, she looked as if she'd seen a ghost.

Sliding into the passenger's side I asked, "What's wrong, Mother?"

"Mia just flashed before me. She's in some kind of trouble." Mom stated before cranking up the vehicle and pulling off. She wasted no time at all driving out of the parking lot.

With my sister being a police, I began to imagine the worst. My mother took every shortcut known to man to get back home. Now bear in mind that cell phones were not popular in the 1980s so just imagine a loving mother trying to get in contact with their beloved child who may be in trouble.

My mother was big time desperate at the thought of a phone call coming to our house as she frantically made a left turn onto Anarchy St. off of American Avenue. She was driving like I've never seen before. We made it to the intersection of Bowery Street and Anarchy St. in no time. Mom continued on Anarchy St. until we reached Metropolitan Avenue. She then made a right onto Voice St. and another left onto the street that our house was on.

As we pulled into the driveway, my two younger sisters were outside in front of the house with some of the neighbors and no one was smiling. My heart sank. I had a flashback of Tall Boy's death when my mother and I left the hospital and arrived at home.

My sisters, Violet and Penelope, rushed to the car. "Mia was in a shootout on Flatbush Ave., in Brooklyn." Violet said.

"What's her condition?" Mom asked as if she already knew my sister was hospitalized.

"She's okay," Penelope stated. "She just bruised her left hand and right knee."

My mother wanted to take a ride to the hospital where Mia was in Brooklyn, but Violet told her that Mia suggested that she just wait for her to call back.

"Everyone, just calm down." I interrupted. "Let's eat before the food gets cold since we know she's okay."

The love of my life was waiting for me at the front door. She looked worried because of the household commotion. I walked through the door, grabbed her hand and asked, "Did you have a good nap?"

Before she could answer, Mom came through the door behind me and said, "Don't have her walking those stairs to the basement." I could tell Mom was still a little shaken because of what had happened to Mia.

"Baby, are you hungry?" I asked.

"No, not right now. You go ahead and eat."

"Okay baby, come sit with me Fabiana." I called out as I was getting set up in my brother's room.

She came into the room and sat on the bed while I turned the radio on. As I opened the container of stuffed shells and meatballs, Fabiana said, "I'll pick at those meatballs."

I had to laugh. "So, sweetie, how was your bus ride here?"

"It was fine."

"Baby, I got to ask…did you run into anybody I had issues with?"

"Why do you ask in that manner of knowing as if you were there?"

"Come on, baby just tell me?"

"Okay, I didn't want to say anything because I knew you would get mad. Anyway, I ran into Black Spades at the bus terminal. All he asked was how you're doing and if we're having a baby. I said yes, we are and that you're doing fine that's all. He then said I wish you both the best and take care. That was it, nothing else."

Allow me to digress for a minute. Black Spades and I had one of the longest one-on-one fights I'd ever known. This was when I was in the eighth grade in IS 747 on American Avenue. We had a beef because Spades was trying to bully a kid from the sixth grade on the second-floor back staircase. While doing so, I sneaked up behind him and punched the daylights out of him.

When he turned in my direction and tried to fight me, he was unable to compose himself. By that time several students had crowded the back staircase, so I decided to embarrass him. I kicked his ass and he tumbled down the stairs. The other students laughed at him as I ran down the stairs and chased him out of the school.

As I recall that was on a Friday. Something told me that wouldn't be the last I'd seen of Black Spades...something was right. I didn't know that over the weekend there would be a war committee with a heavyweight from Graham Boulevard. His name was Gunpowder and Black Spades just happened to be one of his crew members. It was said that Gunpowder smacked Spades around after finding out that I embarrassed him the way I did and ran him off the school premises.

Gunpowder was furious over the whole ordeal, but he knew I was a force to be reckoned with. Now bear in mind the fact that Graham Boulevard crew were allies of the Metro Boys whenever we fought with other crews outside of our neighborhoods, but in this situation Gunpowder demanded Spades fight me one-on-one.

I had no idea until Monday finally rolled around. It was the last period of lunch, and I was hanging out with Fabiana on the first-floor back staircase. We decided to get something to eat from outside. There was a deli adjacent to the IS 747 school yard, and they had some good eats.

Fabiana wanted a grilled cheese with a cup of their delicious tomato soup. I just wanted a bagel with cream cheese and a pint of Tropicana orange juice. I told Fabiana to wait by the back door of the school until I knocked three times in a row. As soon as I walked out the door, Gunpowder, Black Spades, and three of their acolytes marched right past me as if I was a ghost.

I said to myself right there and then that you could not make this shit up. Had I gone back into the school they would have waited for me and probably jumped me. After pondering all factors I decided to walk up the steps right behind them. I walked out onto the school ground, looked Black Spades directly in his eyes and said, "Come on motherfucker, let's fight."

He tried to go toe to toe with me, but that didn't work for him because he was a sloppy fighter. I stayed outside of his awkward flailing and kept throwing straight punches, power punches, uppercuts and hooks with my dominant hand. All Black Spades knew how to do was swing wildly, and in most cases, miss me by a long shot. Occasionally, he would glance toward Gunpowder while running away from me, as if silently pleading for help.

Gunpowder controlled him non-verbally, egging him on to keep fighting and not bear the shame of defeat. I took my time, chasing him as if I was Muhammad Ali. I couldn't say that I fought long and hard because it was quite easy.

However, the fight itself lasted so long that someone from Metropolitan Avenue spotted us scrapping from a BX2 bus in passing and went to Little L and Ethan Lite's house to tell them I was knuckling up with someone at IS 747.

I was so into the fight and beating Spades' ass that I didn't even notice my crew's arrival until I backed off of him to take a puff of my asthma inhaler. At that moment I caught a glimpse of my friend Redd to the left of me. Out of nowhere Little L stepped in front of me with his shirt off and steam coming off of him like he'd just stepped out of a gym. Ethan Lite came from behind, put his arm around my neck, and said, "We here, baby boy."

"Do you want me to finish fighting Black Spades?" Little L asked.

I told everyone to stand down, considering Gunpowder had showed respect. Spades and I went at it for another round. From the beginning, I was in control of the fight. Hell, I even let him get a few licks in. For the rest of the battle I just stayed outside of him and kept jabbing the hell out of him.

I also caught him with a hook to the body and head, knocking him to the ground. He got up fast but a little shaky and then rushed at me out of frustration. He grabbed me and tripped me, and I fell backwards with him on top of me, swinging like a girl.

Both of our crews ran over to pull us apart, and we agreed that that was enough for one day. Afterwards, Gunpowder offered a handshake, which I accepted.

He said, "Now I know you're not a slouch."

My crew and their crew went our separate ways. Most people who remember that particular bout say it was the longest fistfight I'd had in Bronx, New York, behind enemy lines. Although we weren't on each other's turf, I was outnumbered for most of the fight. We had gone at it for at least an hour and forty minutes.

After Fabiana and I finished eating we just chilled, listened to music, and talked. While we were chatting a song came on the radio called *The Metropolitan Beat* by Butter Love and Cool T. I jumped up and started dancing like I was in a disco.

Fabiana shouted at me, "Watch my stomach, you fool."

"Easy baby girl, this is our neighborhood song." I said. While I was entertaining her, Mia finally called from Kings County Hospital and spoke to Mom. When she explained what had happened, the horrific details had all of us on the edge of our seats.

22

Shots Fired

Several hours earlier.

While Mia and her female partner were on patrol for their command of the 77th Precinct, a call came over the radio from the 69th Precinct, as a "10 - 85." Mia and her partner clearly heard police officers in a verbal dispute with multiple suspects.

The women fired each other an *oh, shit* expression as they listened to gunshots and officers screaming, "10-13! 10-13! Shots fired! Officer down!" coming over the police radio. Responding units frantically questioned, "What's your 20?! What's your 20?!" meaning their location.

"Flatbush Avenue and Beverly Road! Caribbean Restaurant!"

They were one block away. "Hang on." Mia warned her partner as she hopped the sidewalk with her police car to avoid traffic hold-ups. They cut through the rear parking lot of Sears department store intending to go onto Beverly Road. Unfortunately, there was a tractor-trailer in a jackknife position attempting to line the oversized vehicle up for a delivery at a loading dock—obstructing their path.

Mia and her partner jumped out of their patrol car and ran towards the gunshots that were still echoing down the street. Once they made it onto the sidewalk, they noticed a car with three Jamaicans sporting dreadlocks fleeing the scene in a vehicle. As they fled they fired at a couple of police officers that had been pinned behind parked cars on Beverly Road near Flatbush Avenue.

The Jamaicans raced straight toward Mia and her partner who had their blue steel .38's already in hand. They simultaneously raised their weapons and fired at the suspects' vehicle. After releasing several rounds, they heard one of the suspects screaming in agony. One of them had been shot. The culprits' car came to a brief pause near Mia and her partner, who kept their weapons aimed at the suspects.

They could still hear the injured suspect screaming while another aimed a 9 mm Uzi out the window and shouted, "Ya Blood Clot Babylon Police Man!" and opened fire, spraying bullets with that fully automatic Uzi.

Mia and her partner dove over a car and then crawled under a van while the spray of bullets missed them by mere inches. The suspects' car, riddled with bullet holes, finally sped off. An additional four suspects were running on foot from other officers who were hot on their trails.

Soon after that, the two officers that had been shot were rushed to Kings County Hospital. Their Commanding Officer ordered Mia and her partner to go to the hospital as well to be treated for their minor injuries. While en route, they heard over the radio that three suspects were apprehended with the help of Emergency Services Unit (also known as SWAT), a police dog, and police helicopter.

Two officers had lost their lives that day.

That was the account of the incident which Mother relayed to us later that night after she hung up the phone. Although Mia was okay, I could still see a bit of worry in our mother's face. I had to ask, "How are you feeling?"

"Much better than earlier, but I want you to know the reason I pray every day," Mom said. "Your sister and her partner walking away with only a few scratches is my reason why. That was nothing but the work of God, son. Trust me when I tell you this, my blessings will fall upon my children from my way of preaching and teaching. This is why I don't go to bars and sit in a congregation of the wicked. Swithun English Wright Junior," Mother used my entire name so I would know that I needed to pay attention to what was coming next, "please get back to praying more. It's more important than you could imagine, especially when you have a family. Now, get ready to drop Fabiana off. Her parents are going to call soon. Also, don't be upset with them, because she's eight months pregnant, going on nine. She should not have traveled today, but that's love for you."

I'd long since learned to pay close attention to what my mother said. The statement about a bar kind of stuck out to me. I felt that my mother had enough worrying for one day, so instead of picking her brain about what she said, I just left it alone.

"Fabiana!" I called out, as I descended the stairs. "It's time to go!"

There she was, staring at me like a wounded puppy as if she thought I was in a hurry to get rid of her. I said, "I would like to spend the rest of my life with you, but your parents want you home. They're worried about you."

"What? What did you say?"

I went silent for a second. It just didn't sit well with people when a guy's mother could know and see things before they happened. "Nothing. What I meant was I just got a feeling they're going to call because it's getting late."

And with that, the phone rang. *And there it is* I thought. I asked Fabiana to answer it for me while I was pulling on my jacket.

After the initial "hello," Fabiana switched to Spanish. It was her mother, Miguelina, and she was disappointed with her daughter, as well as with me. Fabiana wasn't bothered by that, and as a song played over the radio, she began dancing and coaxing me to dance with her. She grabbed my face and said, "You better get a car."

"I'm on it, baby, don't worry."

My mother came down the stairs, ready to drive us over to Bowery. Mom reminded Fabiana to take some of the food that we had bought from Al's since there were plenty of leftovers. I put together a doggie bag for her, and off we went.

While Mom drove, I spotted some of the neighborhood crew on the corner of Voice St. and Metropolitan Avenue – Young Born, Wise, and Knowledge. I asked Mom to pull over for a second so that I could say "hello" to my brothers from another mother.

Getting out of the car and exchanging a homeboy hug with everyone only took a couple of minutes. Someone asked where I had been, and they already knew that I had a child on the way because they had seen Fabiana earlier.

"I've been working, fellas, and I got a baby on the way," I replied. "But I will make some time to check my brothers out later on."

"I heard that you are law enforcement nowadays." Young Born said.

"We all have to make a living, my brother. One love!" I shouted as I returned to the car. As Mom continued driving, they waved at the three of us.

During this ride, I reflected on my past struggles and what life would be like moving from here to Long Island. I assumed it would be the ultimate culture shock. As Mom pulled up to a traffic light right before the Long Island train trestle, Fabiana asked, "Was Graham Boulevard where Mad Rapper was from?"

I replied, "Yes, this is where Graham Boulevard and Metropolitan Avenue starts. They run parallel with each other for several blocks."

The light changed to green, and after driving under the train trestle, we made a left onto Bowery Street. Fabiana sat in the back seat while I sat up front with Mom, but we admired each other in the rear-view mirror. I decided to tease her a little bit by asking, "So you like Mad Rapper?"

"Why, yes, because I'm bad, and I like that red oufit he was wearing in that video for *I'm Bad*. And I also love that gold chain he was wearing."

She and my mother laughed—the kind of giggle that

only happens between women. Girl Code, or something. I was losing ground, so I made a comeback.

"So, instead of getting a car and a place to live, you wouldn't mind if I go and buy that red outfit and a gold chain instead?"

They continued laughing, and then Fabiana with her smart self said, "Can you believe this guy, Mama Wright? He has me knocked up, and he's worried about another guy. Please, Swithun, snap out of it." She poked the back of my head.

As we were passing the VIM department store, I said, "Baby, do you remember when the Bowery Boys chased me into VIM?"

"No, baby." She replied. "It was further up Bowery Street."

"They followed us further down before I confronted them, and when you and your brother were clear of getting jumped, I made them chase me towards VIM."

"How could I forget? I was scared out of my mind."

"I outsmarted them with class, my love," I said just before turning on the car stereo and going through some of the stations. Fabiana liked her little girly music, so when I caught the beginning of *It's a Cruel Summer*, one of her favorite songs by Bananarama, she went through the roof.

"Please, please, please leave it there!" She pleaded.

I folded my arms in surrender and left the radio tuned into that station. For the rest of the ride, my future wife playfully antagonized me by tugging my shirt and patting my cheek, while singing "It's a cruel, (cruel) cruel summer, leavin' me here on my own. It's a cruel, (cruel) cruel summer…" The whole thing seemed to entertain my mother.

As we pulled up to Fabiana's house, she gave my mother a kiss on the cheek and I told her that I would be right back.

I got out of the car with Fabiana and knew exactly what was in store for me. Her mother was waiting at the door, and she didn't look pleased. We greeted each other in Spanish before she welcomed me in. Fabiana translated for us while we spoke. Ms. Miguelina told Fabiana to tell me that she would not allow Fabiana out of her sight anymore while she was pregnant, and that for now I was welcome to sleep over if I wanted to. After thanking Ms. Miguelina, I said I would be over on my days off.

"I expect to hear from you everyday one way or the other" Fabiana firmly communicated.

"Of course, my love!" I replied.

I kissed her mother's cheek before hugging and kissing my lady, as well.

Once back in the car with my mother, she stated, "That's just the tip of the iceberg, son."

"Okay...what am I headed for with her family?"

My mother laughed. "Not much other than the fact that they are a tight family."

"That doesn't tell me much, but I'll just roll with the punches."

During our ride back home, Mom stayed on me about worshiping the Almighty and studying the *Book of Job* more often. All I could do was humbly agree.

As the days went by, I kept my promise to connect with Fabiana daily and visited as often as possible. Within three weeks, I was able to purchase a special edition red Buick from a friend of my brother, Freddie. I don't recall the year, but it was in mint condition.

Having my own vehicle made things around the house a

lot easier since I didn't have to bother Mom to drive me back and forth to work. It also gave me the freedom to be with Fabiana every chance I got. I enjoyed just driving around my neighborhood, but was more than thrilled to take my brother, Amell, and his new girlfriend, Erica, to her family's home in Brooklyn. Erica didn't live too far from where we went to high school. I had the pleasure of meeting her family who were some of the warmest people I had ever met. Her father's name was Alex, and her mother's name was Samantha. Erica had four gorgeous sisters named Carmen, Carol, Miriam, and Amor. Their way of welcoming us was like something out of the movies. I mean, their level of class was colossal. My brother decided to stay over with Erica, and I was invited to stay for dinner.

Alex passed me a cold beer and said, "Have a seat, Swithun." As I made myself comfortable, he said, "So Swithun, what kind of work you do?"

"I am a Peace Officer for NYRA. We cover Speedway, National, and Stars Race Tracks."

"That's a great job, my brother. I work for the New York City Transit Authority."

"How's that going, Alex?" I asked.

He smiled. "Well, you can't beat the benef its from the city."

"This is what I am hearing. One of my sisters is a New York City police officer."

"Is that right? How long has she been on the job?"

"Not too long. A year or so, Sir."

"That's a dangerous job, my friend," he cautioned with concern in his voice.

"You're telling me. She's already had a close call with the Jamaican posse in Flatbush." I said. At that moment, his wife announced that dinner was ready.

"Come on let's eat and finish talking at the table," Alex suggested as we headed toward the dining room.

Boy, did they spoil me with a delicious Puerto Rican dinner. There was a dish called Arroz con Gondules, pasteles de masa con cerdo, a traditional Puerto Rican Christmas dish, and Alcapurria, along with Coquito. Coquito tastes like a delicious coconut shake with a splash of Bacardi rum, and once that drink hit my system, the conversation started to f low very smoothly.

We really had a great evening getting to know one another, and I was told by Erica's family that their home was my home— I was welcome at any time. I didn't want to cut the night short, but I had to make roll call the next morning, so I got a hug and kiss from all the ladies in the house, shook Alex's hand, and said goodnight to everyone.

"Don't be a stranger, we're family now." Erica's sister, Amor, said with a devilish grin.

"I won't. Good night, everyone," I concluded, on my way out the door.

After I started the car and turned on the radio, I drove up Linden Street until I reached Cypress Avenue. I then took the right turn that would lead me to the Inter-Borough Pkwy. East exit, which eventually connected to the Grand Central Pkwy.

As I was pulling into my driveway, I spotted my mother in her bedroom window smiling down at me. Upon entry, I headed straight upstairs. Just as my foot reached the second-floor landing, Mother said, "What are you so happy about?"

I played it cool. "What do you mean, Mother dearest?"

"Swithun, you have more than enough on your plate." She blurted out.

"I know, but I'm just saying Erica has some beautiful sisters, especially Amor."

"You already have a wife."

"Ain't that the truth. And I love and cherish her."

"Then keep it that way, and watch your mind."

"Okay, Mommy. I have to shower and get to bed."

"Before you hit the sack I have to talk with you."

"All right, Mom, no problem. Be right with you."

I kind of knew what she wanted, but I thought I'd let her tell me rather than pushing too much. So, after taking a hot shower and preparing my uniform for the next day, I headed back to her bedroom.

"Yeah, Mom, what's up?"

"Remember what I said to you about congregating with the wicked?"

"Yes, I do. You're not talking about the people I met tonight, right?"

"No. I'm saying in general."

"Yes, Ma'am. Good night, Mom. Love you." I concluded, before kissing her forehead and slipping out of the room.

I wasn't getting off that easy. She called after me, "Swithun...*Book of Job.*"

"Will do, Mommy," I said. She just wasn't going to let that go.

23

Stay Righteous

The sun shone brightly and there was a gentle breeze as I drove up Jerusalem Turnpike towards Metropolitan Avenue on my way home from work the following evening. Although conscious of the road, my mind veered off in another direction as I recalled what I had read in the *Book of Job* the night before. It wasn't that I deliberately pulled those words back into my brain, but more so that they insisted on being there.

...There the prisoners rest together; they hear not the voice of the oppressor...shall mortal man be more just than God? Shall a man be more pure than his Maker?

I tried to deviate from the Scriptures that kept flashing before me, not with the intent to disrespect the Lord, but because I was unable to comprehend why my head had become a dwelling place for those passages. They continued to overtake my brain as I approached Voice St.

Call now, if there be any that will answer thee; and to which of the saints wilt thou turn? For wrath killeth the foolish man, and envy slayeth the silly one.

Near Voice St. and Metropolitan Avenue, with my left turn signal on, I spotted a familiar face behind the steering wheel of an oncoming vehicle that was also making a left turn. He was in full uniform. *Who is this cop?* I wondered.

We stared at each other while we completed our turns in opposite directions. He was in full uniform just as I was. It was my boy, Little L. We both slammed on our breaks, pulled over, jumped out, and ran together for a brotherly hug. We were both speechless at the sight of the other in uniform.

I finally spoke. "I thought you were a police officer when I first gained sight of you, but now I realize you're with the Department of Corrections."

"Just what the hell are you with a horse on your shoulder and NYRA?" Little L asked.

"I'm a Peace Officer for the New York Racing Association."

"Wow. You have Peace Officer status like us."

"Yes, my brother," I answered. "I had to step it up a bit."

"I'll say you stepped it up a lot, my brother, and I'm proud of you." He complimented.

"Thanks, L. It wasn't easy."

I hadn't seen my boy in a little while, and it felt great to be just shooting the breeze with a good friend.

He said, "Oh, before I forget to tell you, Ethan is home."

"Big Ethan? Get out of here!" I was overjoyed.

"Yes, and he's been bodyguarding Mad Rapper for a little while now."

"That's hot L! Really, my dude?"

"Mad Rapper also shouted him out in one of his songs called *Kanday*," L told me.

"How does that song go?" I asked, which prompted him to sing.

"I feel good about Kanday…"

"All right, I'll check it out," I said before I switched subjects. "Me and Fabiana have a child on the way."

"Wow, my brother. So do I, with green-eyes Tracy."

"Life is something else L. How far along is your lady?"

"Any day now."

I smiled. "God bless you and your family, L."

"Same to you, Swithun, I'll stop by some day."

"You're always welcome L. Take it easy."

"You do the same, my dude," He replied, and we went our separate ways, feeling the kind of warmth that can only come from an excellent unexpected encounter, and hearing such good news.

I was in for yet another surprise when I finally arrived at home. As I made it through the door, my oldest sister, Isabella, was sitting at the dining room table—in a New York City Police Academy uniform!

"Hey, sis, I don't recall anybody telling me that you were going to become a police officer, too."

"I have only two months left in the Academy, Swithun." She smiled proudly.

"Cool, Isabella. Freddie is on the list for the Department of Corrections and the Department of Sanitation."

"Wow, go Freddie! Which one do you think he'll go for?"

I shrugged.

She added, "If he's smart, he'll take Corrections. Baby bro, I have to study now."

"No problem, sis, love you. I'll go check on Mom." I told her before running upstairs.

Mom was watching a program on TV. Without turning her head, she said,

"Hi, my son. How did it go today?"

"It went okay at work Mom."

"But...?" She asked.

"On my way home some of the Scriptures I read last night started flashing through my head. They just kept coming."

"Our Father in heaven works in mysterious ways. The more you seek the Lord, you're going to see the gift you have been granted increase."

"Mommy, this is getting scarier and scarier."

"It shouldn't happen with you. You had the knowledge and wisdom at age thirteen to comprehend. And that's along with my preaching and teaching. Embrace it son, for your soul has been in battle even before you were conceived. I know I have told you this before, Swithun, but you have been chosen to go through what you're going through spiritually. This is my reason for telling you to read the *Book of Job*."

"And I have, Mother."

"What have you learned, so far?" Mom quizzed.

"To stay righteous, no matter how much Satan comes after me."

"That's right, son. It's that simple. Serve your Master, and you'll see someday you'll have a testimony to share with the whole world, my God-fearing son."

"That would be something, Mother, after all I have been going through." I humbly answered.

"I may be dead and gone when it takes place, but this is what I am told by the spirits of thee. By the way, Swithun, Ethan called for you. He got the number from Redd. Now

I know he's your friend and all, but his life is his and yours is yours."

"Mommy, please understand that this brother did time for me, and never said a word about me to the authorities. I love Ethan like my own brother."

"Son, I'm not pointing my finger at anyone. I just want you to know your life is heading in a different direction from his. I heard about the fame he has going with that rapper. What's that boy's name again?"

"Mad Rapper, Mommy."

"Yeah, it's just that in that business when there's conflict during the course of him bodyguarding, someone can also follow him back home. Considering you guys are tight, I know you will help him if he's in trouble with someone."

"Ain't that the truth, Mommy."

"I know you, Swithun. You're my son, and you have a heart of gold, but you have a child on the way. It's not like the rumble you guys had with the Bowery Boys. Because that was unstoppable, it was coming like a locomotive train. Heck, I could even say that it was written as a chapter in your life as one of God's warriors. Swithun, when you do something it's always with your whole heart, but like I've said to you on many occasions, we cannot save the world, son. One other thing Swithun before you run off. You say you love Ethan like a brother?"

"I do, Mommy. You know that."

"Then pray for him every day when you think about him, and the good he has done for you."

"I will, Mom, for sure."

"You may go now. Your friend said he will call back a little later."

"Okay, Mommy. Love you. We'll talk later."

"Oh, what do you think about your sister, Isabella?"

"That's a beautiful thing, but I don't even remember anyone saying that she was going to become a police officer."

"This is just the beginning, Swithun, just the beginning." She smiled.

"Good. Well, I'm going to take a shower and relax."

On my way back down the stairs, memories of Tall Boy came out of nowhere and weighed heavily on my mind. I remembered hanging out in some of the places we used to frequent like Rome Park, cousin Timmy's, and others. I quickly sank into an emotional funk and missed him so deep inside my heart. People's physical bodies come into this world and then leave it, but maybe their spirits and the essence of who they are and how they impacted our lives live on forever. They dwell inside our own hearts and souls, vibrant and alive and leaving a gaping hole to f ill in their absence. I missed Tall Boy something awful.

I hurried down to the basement to gather some things and then went back up to take a shower. With warm water pelting me, a memory of the first time I tried marijuana rushed over me because it had been with Tall Boy and Carl Blue in Auntie Cheryl's basement. After a few drags, my cousin and Carl Blue were cracking jokes on me because I couldn't handle it like they could.

To make matters worse, they passed me a lit cigar that Carl had won as a prize from Great Adventures and asked me to take a toke off it, but when I did I quickly realized that I was sucking on the wrong end of the cigar. My lips were sizzling. Tall Boy and Carl Blue fell out laughing.

So now, there I was laughing under the downpour of the shower...and then sobbing because they were both dead.

You know how Tall Boy met his demise, but Carl Blue

was another story. Over the years Carl had found himself in a world of drug dealing and thuggery. It all came to an end when he made a direct sale of crack cocaine to an undercover NYPD narcotics officer right on Clear Avenue in Bronx, New York. He ended up getting a sentence of three years in prison. Once he served his time, he returned back to the streets and did the same old thing. The younger crowd that was dealing on Clear Avenue had respect for Carl Blue, but mostly out of fear. He had a reputation from the years prior, so he had a few of them working for him.

Carl Blue could be pretty hard on them when they came up short with his money. One of them who feared him the most owed him a lot of money because someone had stolen his stash that was under a nearby garbage can. His name was Kirby, and most say he was not built for the drug game considering how young and innocent he was.

Carl Blue gave him a deadline to meet. On the evening that deadline came, he told Kirby to come up to Clear Avenue. Kirby did so, but when he showed up it was like a ghost town. In fact, they were the only two people out on the entire avenue.

Kirby had slowly approached Carl Blue and pretended to have his money, but when he reached into his pocket, he came out with a gun instead, and raised it to Carl's Blue face. Panic-stricken, he turned and made a run for it. He cut across Clear Avenue, but Kirby took aim and fired one shot, hitting Carl Blue in the back of his head, killing him instantly.

Another friend gone. Just like that.

After showering and bleeding in my soul from this emotional rollercoaster ride, I got dressed and took a drive over to Rome Park. I felt driven to take a walk through the woods. As I approached the trails we used to ride our bikes on, I thought, *Damn, this park never did feel like three hundred and fifty-eight acres of land when we were just children.*

As I ventured further into the woods, it became a little darker except for a few patches of sunlight filtering through the trees. I finally reached the hill that Rha Rha was standing on when he was staring up at the sky, and thought, *Was this our playground? Was it, really? Then why do I feel so sad and abandoned here?*

More tears began to fall as that old friend of mine, the presence of death feeling, rolled back into my life. I tried to reason with my Lord, by speaking in my loudest tone, "My God! I suffer from survivor's guilt when I look back on my life, and it hurts a lot, Father! I know this is overall Your battle, my Lord, but I'm starting to weaken. I'm in desperate need of Your strength. I am about to be a father, for crying out loud!" The tears continued to fall as I sat on a huge rock.

Two small woodchucks popped out of nowhere and began chasing one another. I watched them for a few seconds, and had to smile, in spite of myself. I said, "Is that your answer, Father?" I wasn't sure what it meant, but watching these frolicking little critters effectively lifted my spirits. At least for that brief moment.

After driving back to the house, I just wanted to be alone, so I tried my best to enter quietly. My mother shouted from upstairs, "Ethan called again and left you a phone number to call him back!"

So much for sneaking in. "Okay, Mommy," I replied as I continued on to the basement.

The awful presence of death vibe was back, not only overwhelming my body but my mind as well. I began overthinking and wondering what tragedy was near and who it was coming for this time. While laying back on my bed, I heard someone come down the stairs and walk across the living room floor above me. Then I listened to the footsteps making their way to the basement door and down the stairs.

"Who is it?" I shouted, but got no answer.

Mom eventually appeared. "Are you okay, son?"

"Not really, Mom."

She grabbed a chair from the table and sat down. Her expression revealed that she sensed and felt my pain. "Son, you are plenty young and have your whole life ahead of you. I told you once before, you cannot save the world. What's going to be, Swithun, is going to be. Some things are not going to change with others."

"Mommy, I'm heartbroken just knowing that I can feel others' pain and sorrow; Their happiness and sadness. I even know when someone's death is near but don't know who it's going to be, so I can't warn them. At times I say to myself, 'what's the use of my gift?' Mother, when this bad vibe starts to come on it's like a water hose connected to a fire hydrant, and when the tragedy is near it is on full blast. Kind of like the epitome of anxiety... I see ghosts at work. I am a fucking haunted child, for Christ's sake." I rambled on, as I sat on the edge of my bed with a fistful of tears.

My mother shouted, "Don't you blaspheme in this house!"

"Sorry, Mother, but just when I thought things were getting better, I started feeling bad."

"Things are getting better. You'll see that this week. Keep praying, Swithun." She pleaded.

"I will, Mom. Could you at least tell me what's coming? Because I know you know."

"Others have to live for themselves, son," Mother

replied. "And God allows me to see what I need to. Also, you have to realize that you have other siblings, as well. My focus is on all of you. If I see something involving people you know, I'll tell you." Mother stood and headed back up the stairs.

Well...fair enough, I thought. I turned on the radio and caught one of my favorite songs, *Black Butterfly*, by Denise Williams. The song soothed me like a lullaby putting me to sleep.

I awakened a couple of hours later to the song *Heat Wave*. Night had fallen and it was pitch black in the basement, so I had to fumble around a bit to locate the lamp switch. Once I did, I headed upstairs with intentions on going to the bathroom and finding something to eat. Up on the second floor, my mother told me that Fabiana had called.

"Okay, Mom. It's late, so I'll call her in the morning."

"All right son, and sooner than you know it, you two will have your hands full with a gift from God."

As I opened the door to the bathroom, I replied, "I know, Mommy."

While in the bathroom, I couldn't help but notice that bad vibe was still riding me. As I came out, I bade my mother goodnight and headed down to the main floor to f ind some food.

That presence of death feeling haunted me while I warmed up some leftovers and ate. To tell you the truth, I dreaded even leaving the house, but I knew I would have to just man up. Afterward, I went back down to the basement and fell asleep, only to be thrust into a wicked dream about one of my enemies.

I dreamed that Kristan and I were face-to-face on school grounds in the night. The weirdest thing was that the neon lights on the school property only shone upon him and I. Neither one of us spoke. It was just a stare-down. In my dream, I wondered why there wasn't any movement outside until Kristan started to mumble something, but had trouble opening his mouth. Once he did, his eyes turned red, and his teeth were so utterly rotten that they started to fall out of his mouth and onto the ground.

I couldn't wake up fast enough from this horrible dream. When I did, I was drenched with sweat wondering what battle would come next and if it would be my last. A glance at the clock told me that it was 3:10 am. I had to be at roll call at 10 am. I fell back to sleep and woke up late.

24

Birth and Death

After getting dressed and saying bye to Mom, I peeled out of the driveway and headed to Speedway Race Track. By the grace of God, I made it to work five minutes early, just before roll call. Other than that lousy vibe haunting me, my day ran pretty smoothly. Break time rolled around, but I had no appetite. I just wanted to be alone so I found a secluded area where I could hang out away from any crowds.

While sitting on a bench, I recited the Lord's prayer with hopes of finding some refuge in that. At the end of the prayer, I started to drift into a deep sleep as if I hadn't had any. In a dream-like alpha state, I opened my eyes and saw myself floating on a white cloud. A voice within the cloud said, "A child is born, Swithun." As I drifted out of that state, my body swayed back and forth a little.

Near the end of my break, I headed back to my post to f ind Sgt. Baxter covering it. When she saw me she smiled, but her smile promptly turned into a frown when she glanced down at my feet.

Sgt. Baxter spoke sternly, "Wright, congratulations on becoming a father, but don't you ever wear white socks with your uniform again."

"Yes, ma'am," I replied.

"I assume you'll be headed to the hospital after 1800 hours. Be sure to stop at home and change out of your uniform, for liability purposes."

"Yes Sgt. Baxter," I replied.

"Once again, congratulations, Wright. And am I clear on changing out of uniform?"

"Yes, ma'am," I smiled, awkwardly.

"Okay, carry on." She said, before marching off.

I glanced down at my feet. How freakin' embarrassing. That's what I got for rushing out of the house to make it to work on time. And then it struck me.

I was a father! That vision, if I could have called it that, was a glimpse into real-time reality. If not, why would anyone have called my place of employment with the message about the birth of my child? Although dreading the worst because of the bad vibe I was getting, this news filled me to overflowing with joy. My emotions roared like a riptide with the good racing up over the bad, but neither negating the other. In any case, I couldn't wait for my shift to be over so that I could hurry to the hospital to see the love of my life and meet my newborn son.

While anticipating the last few minutes of my shift ending, I began to pray for safe passage in and out of Bronx General Hospital. I had reason to be concerned because it was on the borderline of the Bowery Boys and the Metro Boys turf.

With the new job and all, I couldn't just carry a firearm when I wanted to unless authorized by my employment, but I was too new for that to happen. *But,* I thought, *I am law enforcement. I can always make a call to the local **PD** and get some backup—assuming I can make it to a phone in the middle of a battle in the first place.* My God. I wondered if my imagination was running away with me and if I was becoming unduly paranoid because of that presence of death feeling, and my essential habit of always being on the lookout for signs of trouble.

My shift finally came to an end, and I beat it out of there taking every shortcut imaginable to get home fast. All the while I was wondering, *Did I or did I not already tell Fabiana what I wanted to name our son?* I already had my mind made up. He was my son. He would carry my name.

When I pulled into the driveway, Amell and Erica were on their way out. They congratulated me with hugs, and explained that they would have gone to the hospital with me, but they were in a rush to get to Brooklyn.

"That's fine, bro. Don't worry, you'll see your nephew once he's home—and I am in a bit of a rush myself."

They went on their way, and I blasted into the house. Once through the front door I shouted "hello" at Mom and raced towards the basement to grab a change of clothes and shower gear. As I ran back upstairs I encountered my mother in the hall, laughing at me.

"Take your time." She said. "They'll be there when you arrive."

I give her a quick kiss and an "Okay, Mom," and still bolted to the shower. I was in and out in less than five minutes, then I sprinted out the door and headed to 82-68 Storm St., Bronx, NY.

When I arrived at the hospital, I spotted a familiar face in the visitor's parking lot. It was my buddy, Alfonso Sancho. He approached me wearing a broad smile as I got out of my car. "Where the hell you been?"

I answered, "I've been working at the race track."

"You still work there with the horses?"

"I still work there, but now I'm a Peace Officer."

"Yo, that's amazing, my brother."

"So, what are you doing here?" I asked.

Alfonso's smile drained. "My girlfriend and I had a baby boy a month ago, and he was born premature. He has to stay in the hospital until he's stronger."

It was kind of an awkward moment, dense with both good news and concern. I tried to focus on the good. "Well, congratulations, my brother."

"What are you doing here?" Alfonso finally asked.

"You ain't going to believe this, but Fabiana just gave birth to my son this morning."

"Say word, my dude." Alfonso hauled me in for a congratulatory hug. "This calls for a celebration!"

"Let me go, A" I grumbled good-naturedly.

"I'll come by this weekend, and we'll do something. Alright, Swithun?" He turned and walked away, finalizing over his shoulder, "I'll see you then. God bless you."

"Hey, Alfonso, same to you and your family."

After getting Fabiana's room number and directions to the elevator from the receptionist, I ducked into the gift shop to pick up a dozen roses, a box of chocolates, and a card that read, "IT'S A BOY!"

As the elevator opened right near the nurse's station, I approached a pretty redhead nurse for further directions to

Fabiana's room. She asked, "What is your relationship to Fabiana and her child?"

"I'm the father of her newborn son."

"Follow me," a Jamaican lady said behind me.

When I entered the room and looked at my son, it became clear how they could have been thrown off. Fabiana was sound asleep, but my son was awake, kicking and moving his little arms about. I thought, *Our Father who art in Heaven, You are by far the master of showing off.*

My son was the same exact baby that I had seen in my dream a month before. He was light-skinned just like his mother, and also had her Asian eyes. I picked him up and embraced him, simultaneously admiring his mother as she slept. I had always been madly in love with Fabiana, but at that moment I couldn't put a number, height, width, depth or limit on the love I felt for her and my son because the world just wasn't big enough to hold my love for them.

Fabiana finally awakened, and her first words were, "Are you going to give him your name?"

I sat on the bed holding him and leaned over to kiss her. "What do you think?"

She smiled from ear to ear. "Well, I'm going to give him a nickname."

"And what might that be, my love?"

"Wong. Do you know what that means?"

"No, but I bet you'll tell me."

"It signifies Chinese, because of his eyes."

"Speaking of which, baby, I dug up some history on your mother's country."

"Oh yeah, and what'd you find, Swithun?"

"Panama has one of the oldest Chinatown's in history."

The nurse came back in with some paperwork and asked

if we were ready to register his name. Fabiana pointed at me, and I replied, "Yes, Ma'am! This little prince's name is Swithun English Wright III."

Something nearly sacred unfolded within me as I filled out those forms. The act of registering this child's birth with something tangible and straightforward like pen and paper solidified my relationship to him, to his mother, and even to God. The bond that expanded in those seconds was immeasurable, and I knew how deeply honored I was to have received such a gift from the Almighty. After all I had been through in life I never thought my spirits could be lifted so high, but on this particular day I soared on eagle's wings.

Once I f inished the paperwork, Fabiana asked, "So, how's work, Officer Wright?"

I was shocked. "Who told you?"

"Don't worry about that. I'm smarter than you think."

I thought, *Thanks a lot, Mother.* I couldn't wait to get home to confront her. I should have known that women always had each other's backs.

Fabiana's parents walked in at that moment. Her father shook my hand and gave me a hug. Her mother went straight to Fabiana to see how she was doing and then came over to Wong and I. After giving me a kiss on the cheek, she demanded in Spanish that I give her her baby. Fabiana translated throughout this exchange. Miguelina added that because Fabiana and I could have other children, this one belonged to her.

Miguelina's husband, Pedro, performed a hand gesture that was symbolic of his wife being a little crazy, which drew laughs from everyone.

Mrs. Suarez restated, "I'm serious."

Miguelina inspected her grandson, noticing that he had one ear the same shape as her husband's, and the other one like mine. She also mentioned that in time, he would get some color because of the darkness around his ears. She was elated and very clearly in love with this child. The conversation flowed happily and easily for the rest of the evening until visitation was over.

I thought, *Check out the gift my son came into this world with… he's capable of bringing worlds together.* I gave him and his mother a kiss and hug, and it was time to head home.

I almost hadn't noticed the bad vibe riding me during my visit with my new family. I thought that maybe I should engage in the brighter side of life more often, and pay less attention to that presence of death feeling when it arrived. *Or should I?*

When I got home and was making my way to the basement, I encountered Mr. Jacob Davis. He was as thrilled about my new fatherhood status as I was. He reeled me in for a tight hug. "Congratulations, Rock Hard! How does it feel to be a dad?"

"Jacob, I got to tell you, it's the best feeling on earth. I'm so blessed to have them both in my life."

"I know the feeling, Rock Hard. I'm taking your Mom, your little brother, Ethan, and your little sister, Peanut, with me for the weekend to New Jersey. I miss them every time I'm away at work."

"I hear you, Jacob, I didn't want to leave my new family at the hospital a little while ago," I answered quietly.

"What's this I hear that you don't work with the horses anymore and that you're the law of the NYRA now?"

"Yes, sir, I am." I stood proud and strong.

"So, how's that going for you?"

"I feel important, and it's definitely a step up in pay," I

said. "Not to sound conceited, but I look sharp in a uniform. Overall, I'm just glad to be off the streets and working."

With his right hand on my shoulder and his eyes locked with mine, he said, "Sometimes the streets can haunt you. Be careful where you go and pay attention to what's going on around you."

It had been a while since Jacob and I had spoken because his job kept him away from home so much of the time. I assured him that I would be on point at work and everywhere I went.

Jacob patted me on the back. "Now that's my man. I'll let you go now because I know you have to get ready for work."

"Alright. Thanks for the advice Jacob. I'll see you before y'all go." I hurried down to the basement to gather my things and then headed back up to the second floor to take a shower.

On my way to the bathroom, my mother called me to her door to ask about Fabiana and the baby. I beamed, "Mommy, he's adorable!"

"I bet."

"And Mom, he looks exactly like he did in the dream."

"Well, of course, he does, son. How are you feeling?"

"I feel good, but I still have that bad vibe."

"Remember what I told you about congregating with wicked individuals." She reminded me.

"Yes, Mom, I know."

"Okay, son. We're taking off tomorrow to go to New Jersey for the weekend."

"I know. I spoke to Jacob in the kitchen."

"All right, Swithun. Be careful."

"I will, Mom."

"Okay, good night, son."

During my entire shower all I could think of was Fabiana and my son. With my eyes closed and steaming water pouring over me, I thought, *For their sake I will not jeopardize my life.* I had to stay alive. Even so, the presence of death haunted me, crawling over my skin like some sort of flesh-eating virus.

Afterwards, I went straight to bed and swiftly dove into a dream in which I was headed to the Latin Quarters, my old club spot in Manhattan. While standing in the crowded line-up waiting to be admitted by security, everyone else suddenly disappeared.

In the next instant, the sky opened up to pure daylight as I stood before the door of the club with a bottle of liquor in my hand. Out of nowhere, a huge Kodiak brown bear appeared before me, growling. It began scratching its left paw against the ground as if warning me not to pass the threshold of the door.

I recalled reading about how to react when encountering a bear, so I made eye contact and slowly backed up. It kept on growling and swiping his paw against the ground. I was scared to death and awakened with a jolt. I glanced toward the clock. It was 3:10 am.

I went up to the kitchen for a drink of water before going back to sleep. I woke up on time to kiss and hug my baby brother and sister before they took off for the weekend. Mom and Jacob were pretty much packed and ready to go.

Before they left, my mother said, "Give Fabiana and my new grandson a kiss for me. And you take care of yourself and be careful."

"Okay, Mommy," I replied, "And you and Jacob do the same."

"We'll be fine," Jacob assured me. "See you on Monday, Rock Hard."

"All right, Jacob."

As I watched them walk out of the house, I thought, *As grown as I am, I still feel naked when my mother is not around.* Not to mention that my mind was all over the place because of that bad vibe. It had began to take on the foul stench of a pig rolling around in a pig pen. For some reason, I couldn't shake it. Everything in my body was screaming that death was coming, and really soon. The only question was, would it take me, or would I have to take a life to save my own?

25

Evil Congregation

I arrived at work half an hour before my shift began. Since I had time to kill, I hung out with the rest of the officers who were doing the same thing. The supervisors came out a little before roll call, and to my surprise, I was pulled from my regular post. At first, I thought I was being reprimanded for something. I mean, I had made sure to wear black socks. As it turned out, Sgt. Baxter had a call out, and I was chosen to fill in.

Sgt. Baxter asked me to stand fast after roll call to receive further instructions. After the Captain and Lieutenant addressed all the officers for doing such a good job so far this year, Sgt. Baxter encouraged, "Stay vigilant and keep up the good work. Trackdown Security, you are dismissed from roll call." Sgt. Baxter pointed me out to follow her. "How are your future wife and child?" she asked.

"I can't wait for my shift to be over so that I can go and see them. My son is adorable, and I just love the smell of him."

"Yes, babies are so brand new and fresh. God bless you and your new family, Wright."

"Thanks, Sgt. Baxter."

"Wright, this is your assignment for the day," she said, as we entered the Paddock area. From the Paddock circle, there was a path that led to what looked like a small clubhouse. "Wright, you're going to be working in the Jockey's quarters. You are responsible for these little millionaires. Before each race, you will have a program that sits on the desk you'll be assigned to. It will have the number race that's up, as well as each Jockey's number. You will be attaching these numbers by a safety pin to their left shoulders and checking them all when they go out for a race, and again when they come back from a run. If for some reason a Jockey doesn't return from a race, you'll have to go and see what happened to them. If you encounter a trainer or an owner of a horse being confrontational with a Jockey, you are to step in between them and call for back up immediately. Remember, Officer Wright, these Jockeys are worth a lot of money.

"Yes, ma'am. I understand."

"Okay then, carry on." She turned to march away, paused and added, "One more thing. The shower and sauna are not off-limits if a fight breaks out between the Jockeys."

"Yes, ma'am."

After she left, I took a good look around and muttered, "Holy smokes, is this what it's like to be rich?" The place was very nice. There was a hot tub, a gym, sauna, and a large lounge that was furnished with comfortable couches and tables, and four big-screen television sets broadcasting the races. And then there was the catering—a huge table bearing all sorts of foods and desserts, as well as barrels with ice and soft drinks.

I sat at the security desk for about thirty minutes before "the little millionaires" began trickling in. Anthony Velez Junior, Jose Pena, and Ramon Gonzalez were among them, and they were all true gentlemen who welcomed me with handshakes. Mr. Anthony also told me that I was entitled to help myself to the food.

No disrespect intended toward the other Jockeys, but they, in contrast, weren't so friendly. For instance, Jonas Gleason completely ignored me when I bade him good afternoon. I didn't take it personally because I saw it as just another lesson well-learned when dealing with the rich. Anyhow, it was the coolest assignment for the day, considering I got to eat, sit, and watch each race on TV.

Things were cool until I witnessed a fixed race. A Jockey and his horse got in front of Anthony Velez's horse and blocked him from winning. Once they made it back to the quarters, an argument erupted between them—in the shower—and guess who had to step in between two naked millionaires? Yeah. It was one of the most uncomfortable moments of my life.

After yelling through my radio for assistance a Seargeant whom I had never met before raced right in. He told me, "I have it from here, Officer."

"Yes, Sir," I said and gladly returned to my desk.

After the officer diffused the situation, he approached me to introduce himself as Sgt. Williams Humphrey. He assured me that I had done the right thing in using my radio to call in a supervisor for backup.

Things ran smoothly again until I heard what sounded like someone being choked. I hurried into the men's room to f ind three Jockeys with their fingers stuffed down their throats to induce vomiting.

"Are you gentlemen okay?" I inquired. Their only response was to laugh.

I thought, *What the hell is wrong with these guys?* I soon found out that self-induced vomiting was normal for them. When these little millionaires sat around eating in between races, they'd throw up what they put down to reach their required weight before getting on a horse.

When my shift finally came to an end, another officer by the name of Rick Smith relieved me. I hustled to the main off ice, punched out, and hurried to my car. I wanted to be able to spend a couple of hours with my family, but I had to go home, clean up, and get out of my uniform first.

On the way home, I planned the rest of my evening, being that it was Friday. I decided not to go out with the boys after seeing my family because of the dream I'd had, as well as that horrible vibe. I intended to go to the hospital and then go rent a movie and just chill.

As I pulled into the driveway, I noticed two of my younger brothers sitting outside on the steps. They ran to the car to greet me with smiles. "Redd and Ethan came by for you, Rock Hard."

"Is that right?"

"They had a nice car and lots of gold chains on. Are they rich, Rock Hard? Are they?" my brothers asked.

"Guys, I don't know. All I know is that Ethan is Mad Rapper's bodyguard. That's it. And before I leave for the hospital, you two are coming inside the house."

"Okay, Rock Hard." they replied.

I went into the house to quickly shower and change.

Before leaving, I shouted to my sister, "Penelope, keep Greg and Curtis in the house once I send them in."

She called back, "Okay. Tell Fabiana I love her and my nephew."

"All right, Sis, I have to go."

Upon my arrival at the hospital, a nurse I had dealt with the previous day waved a bottle of milk in front of my face. "You're right on time, Dad."

"It will be a pleasure feeding my prince." I smiled. When I walked into Fabiana's room, my son was awake and quiet, but I could hear other newborns crying throughout the ward. Fabiana was napping. After picking my son up, and hugging and sniff ing him, I fed him his bottle.

Since I had grown up with so many siblings, I didn't have any problems burping Wong after he finished his milk. We sat on his mother's bed for a little while just to enjoy some father and son time before waking her. I would call it a mutual admiration. I couldn't help but notice that the presence of death vibe wasn't as heavy, but still lingered.

After my son nodded off, I continued holding him because letting go wasn't an option. I was hooked on this child. Finally, I kissed his mother's neck, which gently awakened her.

Fabiana murmured, "Isn't that how we ended up with our son?"

"Yes, ma'am."

"How long have you been here?"

"About forty-five minutes. Did your parents come already?"

"Of course. Don't you remember my mother saying that Wong is hers?"

"How could I forget that. Baby, you want any outside food before visiting hours are over?"

"No, Mr. Wright, but tomorrow I would appreciate some Italian food."

I grinned. "No problem, Miss Suarez."

Fabiana sat up to raise the back of her bed, kissed me and said, "Thank you, baby."

"You're welcome, Mama. So, how are they treating you?"

"Not bad. I'd just rather be home already."

"It's only been a day and a half, baby girl. Let's not rush anything. Yours and our son's health is more important than anything."

"I know, sweetie," Fabiana said.

"When are they talking about letting you guys out?"

"Monday or Tuesday, Swithun."

"Okay. That's not so bad. I'll be up here every day for you and our son no matter what."

"You better," Fabiana replied.

We spent the rest of the visit talking about the anticipated move to Long Island. Fabiana's parents weren't feeling it, but I assured her that it would be best for us to get out of the Bronx.

Visiting hours were over before we knew it. I laid my son down in the bassinet after kissing him, and then hugged and kissed Fabiana. "I'll be back tomorrow, my love."

"Okay baby. Good night," She replied.

As I was leaving, I realized that it was too late to go rent a movie, but that was fine because I had some at home. So, I just stopped and picked up some Chinese food on my way.

When I got home, I had no intentions on going back out, except...maybe I'd go get some beer. Maybe. I put on something comfortable and ate while laying across my bed.

And there it was, that bad vibe creeping around me again. I heard a knock at the side door and got up to see who was there by shouting through the basement side window.

It was Floyd and Alfonso Sancho. I let them in and offered them a drink, informing them that I would have run out to get some beer, but they already had something outside in Floyd's car. They suggested that I get dressed, presumably to go out with them. I told them I wanted a drink but really didn't want to go anywhere.

"Come on, Rock Hard. We can just ride and drink what we have in the car." Floyd suggested.

"Okay, but let's take my car." I relented against my better judgment. If I was going to be drinking, I preferred to be in control of my own vehicle and destiny.

We rode around Bronx while sipping on some Olde English 800 beer and Blackberry brandy. Alfonso had me stop at a couple of clubs and bars where he jumped out to go check on the action and girls inside. I waited in the car.

Floyd asked me if I wanted to go in, but I declined, "I don't want to go clubbing in Bronx or Manhattan." I said nothing about the presence of death vibes and the dream I had, fully realizing that not everyone would be comfortable with things of a spiritual or psychic nature. That was my issue, and I was still grappling with learning how to live with it.

Floyd shouted, "Oh, I got the perfect place! It's downtown, Brooklyn. It's a lounge,bar, and restaurant, and they play all kinds of music. It's a sophisticated and elegant crowd, but you can dress any kind of way."

I restated that I didn't want to go anywhere.

Alfonso and Floyd said, "Don't be a party-pooper. We'll just stop in for a little while, have a couple of beers, and leave."

I finally compromised. "Alright fellas. In and out."

We all had a pretty good buzz going from what we had drank earlier, and truth be told, I still wanted another drink so that I could try to suppress this presence of death vibe. But, the deeper we got into Brooklyn, the heavier my vibe became.

We eventually arrived at the Islands Lounge at 1:50 in the morning. There wasn't much of the inner-city crowd in this place. We walked up to the bar and ordered three Heineken beers, and sat back to enjoy them. Unfortunately, the mellow atmosphere didn't stop me from sensing trouble.

Alfonso ordered some finger food which prompted Connie, the Bartender, to ask if we'd prefer a table. We followed her to a pretty good spot at the end of the bar where my line of vision from there to the door was clear, and I would be able to see who came and left.

When Connie brought out the food, I asked her to bring us another round of Heineken's. Alfonso and Floyd were having a good time. They were flirting with some girls at the next table. Floyd realized I was a bit antisocial and wanted to know what was bugging me.

I didn't want to spoil their night, so I played it off and said, "Nothing. Everything is all good."

I tried to interact a little by striking a conversation with the bartender. "This is a very nice spot. How long have you been working here, Connie?"

"I've been working here for about three months now. Where are you from, sweetie?" Connie asked.

"Bronx, baby. What time do you close?"

"At 4 a.m., dear." She replied, and went back to her job waiting on customers.

At 2:30, about ten loud, arrogant guys blew into the place and went straight to the bar. Something angered me...a familiar voice that twisted my face in disgust. It took a minute to place him in my mind. I had a flashback of punching Kristan off his feet in high school. It was him. How could this be? I thought this punk was in prison. The bad vibe I was getting turned up full blast.

I got Alfonso's and Floyd's attention and pointed in Kristan's direction. They were more surprised than I was. Floyd understood my concern and passed me a palm-sized Derringer that held .357 Magnum shells. He said, "Don't worry about anything. We know everyone with him."

I heard my friend, but my gut was warning me that we needed to leave. Immediately. Having two bullets against a group of eight to ten fellas did not comfort me at all because I knew Kristan. Even though it had been a long time, he probably had a gun, and if he didn't, someone with him did.

I stood up and thought about putting my two bullets into the back of Kristan's head with hopes of keeping the rest of his crew from retaliating. I briefly imagined everyone scrambling out of the bar as Kristan's body fell to the ground.

Kristan's back was toward me, as he and his crew raised their glasses. Everyone screamed out, "Welcome Home, Kristan!"

Thoughts of murder consumed my mind. The clanking sound of their glasses as they gave a toast to my nemesis made my body turn away, and my feet carried me to the restroom. The restroom was only a few tables back from where we were seated.

Once inside the dimly lit bathroom, I headed straight for the sink, but splashing my face with cold water didn't alleviate the horrible feeling dwelling in my soul. I glanced into the mirror, and staring back at me was a young boy that I did not recognize. Water dripping from his face and f lames coming out of his eyes sent chills through my body. I began to have a conversation with the old demonic soul that lived inside me. *Rock Hard from the block! Fearless! The young boy who embraced violence. Who sold drugs and carried a gun everywhere, with murder in his heart.*

"If you don't kill Kristan now, he might kill you. You have to kill him. You must!" The young boy with f lames in his eyes demanded.

I pulled out the weapon that Floyd had given me to see how it operated. After briefly examining the gun, the sound of my mother's voice echoed in the hollow, empty bathroom. *"Swithun, watch who you congregate with. Don't forget to read the Book of Job. When you are at war spiritually, alcohol and drugs work in favor of the enemy."* Mother's teachings sounded like a loud bell before I heard Jacob's voice, *"Be careful where you go, and pay attention to what's going on around you."*

I glanced into the mirror, and my face was completely dry. The image of the demonic boy had disappeared. I now saw a clean-cut young man, in uniform. The new me. I had become a new man. I was Officer Wright. The working man. The father of a newborn. A spiritual man who knew better.

I whispered to my new image, "Something bad is about to happen. I have to get out of here. I can't go to jail. My son needs me." Problem was, there was only one way out of that bathroom. One door—and Kristan was on the other side of it.

I had two choices: I could allow the young beast inside of me to kill Kristan, or I could be killed. I recited a quick prayer before stepping out of the bathroom with eyes wide open and my finger on the trigger. Moving toward my table,

I did a quick scan to locate him, while time itself seemed to slow down to a crawl.

I didn't see Kristan anywhere in the bar. As Connie walked towards me with an order for a table near us, I noted that the clock behind the bar read 3:10 – the same time as it had been in my dream with the Kodiak brown bear. At that moment, I knew that I should not have entered a place where the wicked congregated.

"Hey, Connie, is there another way out?" I asked, hoping to avoid a gunfight. I *had* to make it home safely and keep my promise to Fabiana to care for her and my son.

Before Connie could respond, all hell broke loose. A hail of bullets shattered the glass and mirror behind the bar as rapid shots were being fired. I dropped to the floor, along with everyone else around me, including Connie.

Soon, it became apparent that the shots were coming from outside. Connie's head was right beside mine on the floor, but our bodies were lying in opposite directions while shots were still going off. The stench of alcohol seeped into my nose while I became aware of something wet on my sleeve.

Frozen in time and unable to move, I heard Connie whispering frantically, "Hail Mary Full of Grace! The Lord is with Thee. Blessed art thou among women, and blessed is the fruit of thy womb, Jesus. Holy Mary, Mother of God, pray for us sinners, now and at the hour of our death. Amen."

I heard a bloodcurdling scream from a lady nearby, who had been shot in her shoulder. Her scream was absolutely horrible. I heard Connie pleading, "Oh God, please let us make it out of here safely. I promise that I'll never enter a place like this again!"

My thoughts had come out Connie's mouth as we lay on the dirty floor with our heads nearly touching. Something wet and sticky spreading over my torso caused me grab onto my shirt. Blood? Had I been hit? I closed my eyes and began a prayer of my own as the combined sounds of gunfire, screams, and breaking glass continued exploding around me.

"Swithun, don't be in bars congregating with the wicked. You have a family to care for now…"

My beloved mother's warning echoed in my brain just before I blacked out...

To Be Continued...

About the Author

Swithun English Wright Jr. is a Bounty Hunter and a Private Investigator. He has had ghost encounters since he was born.

Printed in the United States
by Baker & Taylor Publisher Services